EYE ON
ART

Mary Cassatt
Famous Female Impressionist

By Rachael Morlock

LUCENT PRESS

Published in 2019 by
Lucent Press, an Imprint of Greenhaven Publishing, LLC
353 3rd Avenue
Suite 255
New York, NY 10010

Designer: Deanna Paternostro
Editor: Melissa Raé Shofner

Library of Congress Cataloging-in-Publication Data

Names: Morlock, Rachael.
Title: Mary Cassatt : famous female impressionist / Rachael Morlock.
Description: New York : Lucent Press, 2019. | Series: Eye on art | Includes
    bibliographical references and index.
Identifiers: LCCN 2018035285| ISBN 9781534566101 (library bound book) | ISBN
    9781534566095 (pbk. book) | ISBN 9781534566118 (e-book)
Subjects: LCSH: Cassatt, Mary, 1844-1926. | Impressionist artists–United
    States–Biography. | Women artists–United States–Biography.
Classification: LCC N6537.C35 M37 2019 | DDC 759.13 [B] –dc23
LC record available at https://lccn.loc.gov/2018035285

Printed in the United States of America

CPSIA compliance information: Batch #BW19KL: For further information contact Greenhaven Publishing LLC, New York, New York at 1-844-317-7404.

Please visit our website, www.greenhavenpublishing.com. For a free color catalog of all our high-quality
books, call toll free 1-844-317-7404 or fax 1-844-317-7405.

Contents

Foreword

What is art? There is no one answer to that question. Every person has a different idea of what makes something a work of art. Some people think of art as the work of masters such as Leonardo da Vinci, Mary Cassatt, or Michelangelo. Others see artistic beauty in everything from skyscrapers and animated films to fashion shows and graffiti. Everyone brings their own point of view to their interpretation of art.

Discovering the hard work and pure talent behind artistic techniques from different periods in history and different places around the world helps people develop an appreciation for art in all its varied forms. The stories behind great works of art and the artists who created them have fascinated people for many years and continue to do so today. Whether a person has a passion for painting, graphic design, or another creative pursuit, learning about the lives of great artists and the paths that can be taken to achieve success as an artist in the modern world can inspire budding creators to pursue their dreams.

This series introduces readers to different artistic styles, as well as the artists who made those styles famous. As they read about creative expression in the past and present, they are challenged to think critically about their own definition of art.

Quotes from artists, art historians, and other experts provide a unique perspective on each topic, and a detailed bibliography is provided as a starting place for further research. In addition, a list of websites and books about each topic encourages readers to continue their exploration of the fascinating world of art.

This world comes alive with each turn of the page, as readers explore sidebars about the artistic process and creative careers. Essential examples of different artistic styles are presented in the form of vibrant photographs and historical images, giving readers a comprehensive look at art history from ancient times to the present.

Art may be difficult to define, but it is easy to appreciate. In developing a deeper understanding of different art forms, readers will be able to look at the world around them with a fresh perspective on the beauty that can be found in unexpected places.

INTRODUCTION

An Uncommon Artist

Mary Cassatt was an unlikely force for change in the 19th century art world. At a time when relatively few women pursued careers as artists, Cassatt was a professional who became recognized and celebrated around the world. Her work brought the modern moment to life, forming a bridge between the art of the past and the art of the future.

As a student, Cassatt received the standard art education of the time. In classrooms, studios, and museums, she closely examined the technical aspects of Western art. She learned to draw and paint like the Old European Masters, using a sharp eye and skillful hand.

Having learned about art of the past, Cassatt was not interested in merely reproducing its effects. Rejecting the subjects and styles of academic art, she pursued a new artistic vision. She would use her mastery of artistic techniques and apply it to modern life. Instead of painting the heroic characters of biblical or historical dramas, Cassatt focused her attention on the daily life surrounding her.

This revolutionary artistic approach was slowly gaining ground, and Cassatt eagerly joined the new movement. She saw an opportunity to make well-crafted art that was related to the historical moment she was living in. Moreover, she was willing to risk her career and reputation in order to pursue it. Motivated by her desire to create groundbreaking, original works, Cassatt joined the Impressionists. The

Many of Cassatt's works focus on women's daily activities. Her female subjects are often pictured reading, sewing, crocheting, socializing, or caring for children.

Impressionists were a group of artists who rejected traditional composition and painted "impressions" of everyday scenes by quickly putting paint to canvas, capturing shifts in color and light with broad brushstrokes.

American in Paris

Mary Cassatt's home in Pennsylvania placed her close to the Pennsylvania Academy of the Fine Arts, where she began her studies. However, even this well-respected school was no match for the educational prospects of European museums and studios.

In 1865, Cassatt began traveling as an art student in France. After several European trips, she settled into life as a professional artist in Paris, France. Cassatt was convinced that Paris was the seat of visionary artistic growth, and she adopted it as her new home. Altogether, she would spend more than 52 years of her life in France.

Cassatt entered Paris during a time of upheaval in the art world. The seeds of change had been sown by the Realist movement of the 1830s and continued into the 1870s with a group of independent artists. This collective came to be known as the Impressionists. The Impressionists boldly experimented with new and radical directions in art.

When Mary Cassatt joined the Impressionists in 1877, she was the only American in their ranks. She would contribute to four of the eight Impressionist exhibitions that forced critics, artists, and the public to reevaluate the form and purpose of great art. She played a major role in the changes that were underway.

Promoting Impressionism

With her unique style, Cassatt drew attention to the Impressionist exhibits. Her own work offered a glimpse into the world of modern women. It pictured women at home, in the garden, at the theater, or visiting friends. This female perspective balanced the scenes of bustling, urban life and country landscapes offered by male artists.

Cassatt's significant contributions to the Impressionist movement extended beyond her role as an artist. Even before she joined the Impressionists, Cassatt admired their principles and promoted their works. She played a monumental role in advising her friend Louisine Havemeyer to begin what would become a celebrated collection of Impressionist art.

This advisory role was repeated with other notable friends and collectors.

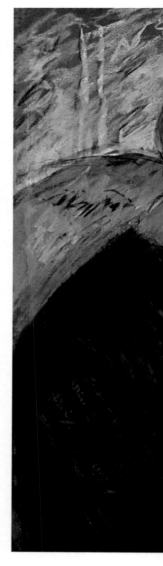

The Impressionist style gave Cassatt the artistic tools to create images such as this hug between a mother and child depicted in pastel. Interactions between women and children defined Cassatt's work.

Cassatt's influence encouraged the sale of Impressionist art, thereby offering financial support and greater freedom to the movement's artists. Her American connections secured a larger market and a wider audience for French Impressionism.

The first Impressionist exhibition in the United States took place in 1886. Many of the private collectors who loaned work to this show were either friends or relatives of Cassatt. The

Cassatt's self-portrait from 1878 shows the beginnings of an Impressionistic style of loose paint strokes and unconventional compositions. Despite her fine hat and clothing, Cassatt's pose is casual.

chain of events that ignited a strong American enthusiasm for Impressionism can be reliably traced back to her.

A Female Artist

Mary Cassatt worked within a world dominated by men. She remained single throughout her life, choosing an artistic career over the duties of a wife and mother. Her own mother wrote of Cassatt's life choice, "After all a woman who is not married is lucky if she has a decided love for work of any kind [and] the more absorbing it is the better."[1] Cassatt's work certainly was absorbing. Her firm belief in her own ability and potential strengthened her pursuit of fame and artistic accomplishments.

Until the recent past, the chroniclers of art history were predominantly male. As a result, the efforts of countless female artists had been effectively erased from art history for many years. In fact, Cassatt had many female predecessors and peers in the arts. Though she was not alone in choosing art as her life's ambition, the extent to which she fulfilled her ambition is extraordinary.

Cassatt used Impressionistic innovations to depict women's lives. Her shared experience and awareness of life as a woman informed her artistic portrayal of them. This resulted in a revolutionary sense that the women and children she represented were subjects rather than objects. Cassatt's humanizing effect, achieved with modern artistic methods, has a timeless appeal.

CHAPTER ONE

Early Life

Katherine and Robert Cassatt were living in Allegheny City, Pennsylvania, when their daughter was born on May 22, 1844. Mary Stevenson Cassatt was welcomed into the family by her parents and three older siblings: Lydia, Alexander, and Robbie. At the time, Allegheny City was a wealthy and bustling marketplace. It was a hub of culture, industry, and transportation, served by both the Pennsylvania Railroad and the Pennsylvania Canal. Across the river lay Pittsburgh, Pennsylvania, the metropolis that would eventually extend to include Allegheny City.

The Cassatt family was highly respected and well established in their community. Robert had great success as a stockbroker and businessman. He was elected mayor of Allegheny City in 1846. Robert's public service and financial success made it possible for him to retire while he was still in his early 40s.

With retirement came a quieter life, and the Cassatt family moved to a country home in Lancaster, Pennsylvania. Mary was four years old when she arrived at their new residence, a mansion called Hardwicke. Between lessons with their governess, the Cassatt children were free to explore the nearby countryside. Mary then became an older sister when her brother Joseph Gardner, often called Gardner or Gard, was born.

As a family of seven, the Cassatts left behind their country life in 1849 for a new home in Philadelphia,

Pennsylvania. They already had many family and social connections in Philadelphia, and they became quickly accustomed to the new city with its greater access to cultural and social events. The Cassatts also sought medical treatment in Philadelphia for Mary's brother Robbie, who suffered from a bone disease. Mary and her older siblings went to school in the city, and the family took advantage of the many excitements of urban life. This stay in Philadelphia lasted about a year and a half. Then, the Cassatts were on the move again, this time to Europe.

Life Abroad

The Cassatt family chose a good year to begin their time abroad. In the summer of 1851, Mary and her family boarded a steamship bound for England. At the same time, the Great Exhibition at London's Crystal Palace was in full swing. The opportunity to visit this grand display of culture and industry may have partly motivated the family's travels. Other reasons for going abroad included the educational interests of their children and Robbie's health. The Cassatts hoped to find more advanced medical care or a cure for their son's disease, which was becoming increasingly serious.

After a month in London, the Cassatts moved on to Paris. They would spend the next two years in this culturally sophisticated city. Mary and her siblings went to school in Paris and became fluent in French. It is likely that Mary studied a variety of academic and artistic subjects such as drawing and music.

Katherine already spoke fluent French, an advantage that likely eased the family's transition to life abroad. In addition to school, Mary's parents introduced her to the cultural offerings that made Paris the center of the art world. Visits to museums and galleries fueled Mary's early interest in art. As the historian David McCullough wrote of seven-year-old Mary, "It would also be said that her interest in painting began then, which would appear to make her the youngest American thus far to have come under the spell of the arts in Paris."[2]

In addition to a rich backdrop of arts and culture, Paris was a site of significant political change. The Cassatts were in the city on December 2, 1851, the day Louis-Napoléon staged a political *coup d'etat* (the overthrowing of a government, often by military means). The event left an incredible impression in Mary's memories of her childhood in Europe. His actions successfully dissolved the existing government and led to his own reign as emperor. This laid the groundwork for changes in Paris that would shape Cassatt's adult experiences abroad.

European Education

After two years in Paris, the Cassatts continued their European tour in the spring of 1853. Germany offered

The Great Exhibition of 1851 set off a trend of world fairs and expositions that would continue throughout Cassatt's life. As an artist, she would exhibit her work at several of these events.

new experiences as well as better educational opportunities for Mary's oldest brother, Alexander. Alexander—or Aleck, as his family called him—

was very intelligent, and his talent for engineering could be best encouraged at a boarding school in Heidelberg, Germany. While Alexander received more specialized instruction, Mary had the opportunity to learn German.

Another year passed, and Alexander was accepted into a technical

At the International Exposition of 1855, Jean-Auguste-Dominique Ingres was awarded the Legion of Honor for paintings in his characteristic Neoclassical style, such as the one shown here. His detailed works were highly regarded.

ANNO 1827

university in Darmstadt, Germany. Once again, the family moved and settled in a new city. However, their plans for life in Darmstadt were cut tragically short. After a 5-year struggle, Robbie died of bone disease at age 13. According to biographer and art historian Nancy Mowll Mathews, 11-year-old Mary was especially affected "since Robbie was the closest to her in age and was her steady companion during the many moves of her childhood. With the loss of Robbie she was forced to become more self-sufficient."[3]

The family had planned to remain in Darmstadt for another year, but under the weight of their loss, they chose to return home to Pennsylvania. Alexander stayed behind to finish school while the rest of the family sailed for the United States.

A final stop in Paris may have allowed the Cassatts to visit the International Exposition of 1855. Inspired by the success of the Great Exhibition, the International Exposition offered visitors a stylish taste of the accomplishments and popular advancements of the day. The new emperor, now known as Napoleon III, seized the opportunity to show off French art and industry. Neoclassical art, inspired by the art and life of ancient Rome and Greece, was proudly showcased in the Fine Arts building.

During this period of grief for the Cassatt family, it is unclear whether they were able to view or enjoy the Exposition. The styles, achievements, and rivalries of this time would shape the artistic climate Mary later inherited. If Mary had the opportunity to see the artwork at the Exposition, it was certain to have left an impression.

Home Again

After living in a quick succession of large European cities and dealing with Robbie's death, the Cassatts sought a quieter location for their new home. Instead of moving back to Philadelphia, they settled in West Chester, Pennsylvania. Over the next three years, they maintained their ties to Philadelphia with frequent train rides to visit the sites and society of the big city. Unlike the Hardwicke mansion in Lancaster, the Cassatts now chose more modest accommodations.

Mary continued her education, by now fluent in both French and German. In addition to her academic pursuits, she was active and athletic. As an adult, Mary's brother Alexander wrote a letter to his future wife describing the pleasures and pursuits the siblings shared in their younger years:

> [Mary was] always a great favorite of mine. I suppose because our taste was a good deal alike— whenever it was a question of a walk or a ride or a gallop on horseback it didn't matter when or what weather, Mary was always ready, so when I was at home we were together a great deal.[4]

In 1858, the Cassatts returned to Philadelphia. They bought a house in their old neighborhood and settled in for the next four years. Philadelphia offered many attractions for Mary as she entered her teenage years. The 14-year-old now lived in the second-largest city in the United States. Until 1830, it had been the largest U.S. city, and in the mid-1800s, it maintained its position as the largest center of industrial production. There, Mary had access to many social, historical, and cultural treasures and abundant opportunities to stoke her interest in art.

Exploring Art

Luck or fate had returned Mary to Philadelphia, home of the most prestigious and progressive art school in the United States—the Pennsylvania Academy of the Fine Arts. Her family's city residence was located only a few blocks away from the Pennsylvania Academy and surrounding artists' galleries and studios, and when Mary

was 15, she eagerly enrolled in an art class there. She submitted her application and registered six months before the class would begin and before any other students. After turning 16, the minimum age for students at the Pennsylvania Academy, Cassatt left behind her general studies and officially began life as an art student.

The Pennsylvania Academy of the

As soon as Mary Cassatt was old enough, she enrolled in art classes at the Pennsylvania Academy of the Fine Arts, shown here.

Female Students

I n Cassatt's class at the Pennsylvania Academy, female students were allowed to view the galleries side by side with male students. However, restrictions were implemented to protect the modesty of female students. After 1856, for example, fig leaves were carefully attached to the casts of nude male sculptures.

Just before Cassatt enrolled, the Pennsylvania Academy opened their anatomy lectures to female students. The study of anatomy formed a basis for understanding the human form. Anatomy lectures sometimes included the dissection of human bodies. This was likely to be a controversial subject for the parents of many female students at this time. It is a testament to Cassatt's forward-thinking parents that she was permitted to study art in such a progressive environment.

The ability to work from nude models remained closed to Cassatt as a student. Nearly 25 years later, her former classmate and artist Thomas Eakins was forced to resign his position as director of the Pennsylvania Academy for challenging this practice. Eakins, who encouraged all artists to work from life, had removed a male model's loincloth in a women's class.

Fine Arts was founded in Philadelphia in 1805. Unlike many European and American art schools, the Pennsylvania Academy opened its doors to women. The works of well-known female artists had been hung in its galleries since the Pennsylvania Academy's first annual exhibition in 1811. In 1844, enrollment was opened to female students. Even more progressively, the segregation of female students at the Pennsylvania Academy was dissolved in 1856. In earlier years, female students had separate days and hours for studying and copying art, especially art featuring nudes. When Mary Cassatt began in 1860, she was able to attend integrated classes with her male and female peers.

The Pennsylvania Academy housed a great number of celebrated works from around the world and hosted frequent events to exhibit them. As a student, Mary had access to the work of selected Old Masters (skilled painters who created their works between the 1300s and early 1800s) and plaster casts and engravings of important works. The works of professional female artists were also on view.

Artistic education at the Pennsylvania Academy was based on two main practices: studying the works of masters and working from live models. When Mary began at the Pennsylvania Academy, live models were not available to female students. Cassatt and her friends organized their own solution. Together, they met for 1 hour 4 days a week, taking turns modeling for each other. To support this practice, the Pennsylvania Academy made a modeling room available to the hardworking students.

In a group of like-minded young men and women, Cassatt made lasting friendships. Her closest relationship was with fellow student Eliza Haldeman. Cassatt and Haldeman spent time in serious artistic study and discussion at the galleries, viewing exhibits around Philadelphia, and visiting each other's families. Surrounded by the art of her predecessors and the enthusiasm of her peers, Mathews asserts that Cassatt would have been confident in her ability to pursue an artistic career:

> Cassatt and Haldeman were well aware that their path would not be easy. They had suffered enough of their male colleagues' patronizing jabs to understand that women artists faced persistent skepticism in the pursuit of their goals, but nevertheless they had enough proof that women could and had made it as artists and enough encouragement to set off on that course themselves.[5]

Civil War

In the spring of 1862, Cassatt finished classes and left Philadelphia for her family's newly built home in the country. From this point on, she worked largely independently, traveling occasionally into the city to study works or receive critiques on her efforts. She maintained strong ties with her peers, especially Haldeman, who remained in the city and at the Pennsylvania Academy for the next two years.

An atmosphere of uncertainty had begun to color the emotions and concerns of the Pennsylvania Academy's students. In 1861, the threat of civil war became a reality. The Cassatts' political views on the war are unknown, although their eventual support of the Union Army, which included many friends, relatives, and acquaintances, is undeniable.

Cassatt's immediate family was spared during the war. Alexander was home with a new degree and working for the Pennsylvania Railroad. Indeed, the railroad's important role in the Union's success during the American Civil War ensured a bright future for Alexander and his profession. Mary's father also experienced financial success at this time. In 1865, he opened a brokerage office in Philadelphia and began work again.

When the war ended in 1865, Mary was 21 years old and more invested in her artistic career than ever. She felt that she had exhausted the artistic possibilities of studying in Philadelphia and working from local models in the country. She was eager to take the next step. For Mary and many of her

In 1862, in the midst of the Civil War, these female students of the Pennsylvania Academy collaborated on a flag. Many women in Cassatt's circle sewed flags or made bandages to show their support for the Union.

classmates, the end of the war signaled the opportunity to venture abroad.

Compared to the museums in Europe, the Pennsylvania Academy's art collection was modest and incomplete. Mary was convinced that her path as an artist must include a period of study in Europe. Persuading her father was another matter. Mary later stated they had had a dispute in which her father exclaimed he would almost rather see Mary dead than pursue her artistic future alone in Europe.

Even for relatively liberal parents like the Cassatts, the prospect of their daughter becoming a professional artist was difficult to handle. Artistic pursuits were respectable for young women as a hobby, but they were less favorable as a career. Haldeman's father predicted that her artistic interests were a passing phase. In a letter to his daughter, he claimed, "You will get married and settle down into a good housekeeper like all married women [and] send off your paints into the garret [attic]! There is a prediction for you, and one founded upon almost universal experience."[6]

Pursuing professional art abroad involved the sacrifice of a traditional life and the risk of a damaged reputation in middle-class society. For

In October 2007, Cassatt's etching **Mrs. Cassatt Knitting, Profile View** *sold for $17,500 in an auction at Christie's, a famous auction house in New York City.*

Cassatt, her single-minded interest in art outranked all other concerns. From this early juncture, she was willing to set aside the possibility of life as a married woman if it meant that art could be the driving force in her life.

Despite her father's disapproval, Cassatt was resolved to go to Europe. It was decided that her mother would join her for the transatlantic journey and help her settle into life abroad. A steamer carried the pair across the ocean, and they arrived in Paris in December 1865.

Studying the Masters

Although Paris was the center of Modern art, Parisian artists were several steps behind in their approach to female art students. In Philadelphia, women were free to enroll in the Pennsylvania Academy of the Fine Arts. In most prestigious European schools, women were excluded as a rule. The premier art school in Paris, the École des Beaux-Arts, was strictly closed to women. Women would not be admitted until 32 years after Cassatt arrived in Paris.

Instead of attending schools, female artists dedicated themselves to the European museums overflowing with masterpieces. In Paris, the Louvre was the ultimate destination for artists. One of Cassatt's first tasks after arriving was to obtain a special permit for copying works in the Louvre. She dedicated several hours every day to studying works that spanned the centuries. She would set her easel in front of a famous painting in order to imitate the composition, color, brushwork, tone, and other qualities, studying how they harmonized into a successful and immortal work. The general opinion among artists was that copying the masters was the best way to gain technical skills.

In addition, Cassatt and her female peers could also seek guidance in private studios. Many established artists of the day operated their own studios for a select group of students. For a fee, students would receive the benefit of the artist's expertise and learn more about their style and techniques.

Women in the Louvre

aytime visitors to the Louvre in the 19th century may have found it difficult to see beyond the swarms of copyists' easels. Cassatt and many other American, French, and international artists crowded the Louvre to study and learn from the Old Masters. Copying the masters was both an educational and economical practice. Many copyists sold their finished works to tourists or completed commissioned copies for patrons.

With so many artists at work, the Louvre became a valued gathering place. The copyists themselves were an important attraction. For some, the social meetings and flirtations provided distractions from the tedious efforts of copying. Haldeman described the social role of the Louvre in a letter to her sister:

> There is a quantity of our old Artist acquaintances over here just now and I am afraid the Louvre will become a second [Pennsylvania] Academy for talking and amusing ourselves ... But as gentlemen cannot come to see us at the Hotel, we are obliged to receive them at the Louvre.[1]

Winslow Homer's 1867 depiction of copyists at the Louvre offered a glimpse into the daily practice of many artists abroad, including Mary Cassatt.

1. Quoted in Nancy Mowll Mathews, *Mary Cassatt: A Life*. New York, NY: Villard Books, 1994, p. 53.

Académie des Beaux-Arts

The Académie des Beaux-Arts, or the Academy of Fine Arts, was established to promote art and artists. Its high standards measured all art against the achievements of the Classical and Renaissance periods. The Académie provided training for artists through the École des Beaux-Arts.

In 1667, the Académie began holding regular exhibitions that were open to the public. This event became known as the Salon, named after the *salon carre*, or square room, in the Louvre where it was held. Jury-selected works were crammed into the exhibition space, completely covering the walls. The best art was granted a distinguished place at eye level. Lesser works were "skyed," or placed high above the other paintings, reaching up to the ceiling.

The French Académie influenced many other European art schools. In order for art to meet the exact standards of "academic" art, it had to imitate the styles, techniques, and subject matter of the classical world. These limitations did not encourage artistic creativity, vision, or freedom. A gradual resistance to the Académie grew throughout the 19th century and eventually led to Impressionism's radical break with the institution.

The Académie des Beaux-Arts is one of the five academies of the Institut de France. The Académie's classical standards for art were quite different than the free and sweeping standards of the Impressionists.

Cassatt was accepted into the studio of Jean-Léon Gérôme, a notable painter. Cassatt's former classmates in Philadelphia were impressed that she had secured a place with such an illustrious artist.

As she had done with her early enrollment at the Pennsylvania

Academy, Cassatt was ahead of many of her classmates. Six months after her arrival, Haldeman, Eakins, and several other classmates from Philadelphia joined Cassatt in Paris. After the Civil War, more than 1,800 American artists came to Paris to study and work.

Eakins also began studying at

Gérôme's studio, while Haldeman entered the studio of portrait painter Charles Joshua Chaplin, who held a special women's class. A brief disagreement separated Haldeman and Cassatt. Cassatt had a tendency to freely share her strong opinions, often at the expense of others' feelings. However, Cassatt and Haldeman reconciled their differences, and Cassatt also joined Chaplin's studio.

By this point, Cassatt's mother had already returned home. She left her daughter to try her luck and skill in navigating the art world of France. Within a close circle of American students, Cassatt was well equipped. She also possessed a guiding artistic passion and the financial backing of her parents to support her. Cassatt wholeheartedly embraced this first period of independence in her adult life.

French Lessons

In addition to urban attractions, France offered artistic opportunities in the countryside. Artists' colonies with distinctive, nature-focused styles sprang up outside Paris. Cassatt and Haldeman boldly toured rural France to visit them.

In February 1867, the pair of friends set off for Courances, a small French town southwest of Paris. There, as Haldeman wrote, "Everything is in the most primitive style."[7] For the first time, they encountered the customs and amusements of the French countryside. Instead of life with sophisticated Parisians, the Philadelphians found themselves in country homes touched by poverty. Sanitary and social practices were more relaxed. Living among people of modest means was a new experience for Cassatt and Haldeman. Haldeman's descriptive letters to her family convey a sense of her unfamiliar and rustic surroundings:

The cottages of the peasants are also very romantic, we were painting in one today. It is several hundred years old, the rafters are all bare black and wormeaten. The old chimney was beautiful and we were entertained with the music of a spinning wheel and the ticking of a clock ... The folks were very kind and brought out some pancakes to regale us on. They were laid across the tongs to warm and then the old woman (75 years old) handed them to us in her hands. I eat one mouthful for decencys sake and then put the rest in my pocket when they were not looking and said it was good![8]

Courances was not far from a colony of artists in the village of Barbizon. Painters in the Barbizon school painted in and near the Forest of Fontainebleau, studying nature for landscapes and genre paintings. At the time, genre painting took daily life as its subject matter. The seasonal work of peasants and their quaint country customs were popular themes. As insightful observers, Cassatt and Haldeman would have noticed that these idealized views glossed over the dirt, poverty, and disease that were characteristic of rural life.

Jean-François Millet was the Barbizon's most famous genre painter. His work portrayed simple scenes of peasant life in serene country settings. Cassatt and Haldeman visited Barbizon to learn from Millet and the landscape artists. However, the relaxed practices of the Barbizon school, and of Millet in particular, were uninspiring to Cassatt. Haldeman recorded "the horror we were seized with on hearing he painted without models."[9]

In April, Cassatt and Haldeman tried their luck at another artists' colony in Écouen, France. Several fellow American painters were already installed there, along with the notable French painters Pierre-Édouard Frère and Paul Constant Soyer. The example and free advice of "the most celebrated Genre painters in France,"[10] as Haldeman called them, were greatly valued. After absorbing the lessons of rural painters, Cassatt and Haldeman joined the annual migration into Paris for the opening of the 1868 Salon.

Acceptance and Success

The opening of the Salon was the artistic event of the year in Paris. A jury from the Académie des Beaux-Arts reviewed thousands of submissions. The work that passed their inspection was hung at the Salon. Artists, critics, potential buyers, and the general public attended and engaged in lively discussions about the featured artists. The success of an artist among the elite art establishment in France depended on their inclusion in the Salon.

Before leaving for the country, Cassatt had submitted one of her finished paintings to the Salon jury using her middle name, Stevenson. To her surprise and delight, *The Mandolin Player* was selected and exhibited in the Salon of 1868. The figure study depicted a young girl holding her instrument, a familiar subject at the time. The painting's style dutifully borrowed from the Old Masters' tradition of using a dark background and shadowed effects.

Haldeman also had a painting accepted, and she and Cassatt excitedly used their special artist's passes to enjoy the exhibit with friends. The two young women had accomplished an impressive and necessary step in pursuing serious artistic careers.

After the excitement of the Salon, Cassatt returned to the country. She visited another French artists' colony in Villiers-le-Bel, where Haldeman eventually joined her. Cassatt stayed there through the winter, taking instruction from the artist Thomas Couture. A controversial and rising figure in the art world, Édouard Manet, had also studied under Couture.

Jean-François Millet frequently displayed simple scenes in country settings in his paintings. One of these famous scenes, The Gleaners, was painted in 1857 and is shown here.

Couture's style was looser than the popular art in Paris. His student Manet applied this fluid style in depicting unconventional modern scenes. Together, Couture and Manet's work helped spark the Modernist movement away from academic art, which is likely to have attracted Cassatt's attention.

After another year of preparation and study, Cassatt was disappointed that her 1869 Salon submissions were rejected. She returned to Paris and recommitted to copying at the Louvre. However, her characteristic desire to travel led her away again after a few months, this time to the Alps with an American friend. They traveled and sketched, staying in small villages. "We are roughing it most artistically,"[11] Cassatt wrote to Alexander's new wife back in Pennsylvania.

Cassatt's ties to her home and family in Pennsylvania depended entirely on the exchange of letters or messages and gifts delivered by traveling friends. By 1869, Cassatt had been in Europe for four years and had not seen any of her family members. She had lost her closest link to home when Haldeman returned to America the year before. Finally, in December 1869, Cassatt's mother met her in Paris for Christmas.

La Musique
1874
Huile sur toile
Paris, Petit Palais, Musée
des Beaux-Arts de la Ville de Paris

A 2018 exhibition in Paris of Cassatt's work showcased several early masterpieces, including **The Mandolin Player** *(far right). Cassatt burned most of her early work, leaving few examples of her style before Impressionism.*

Franco-Prussian War

The Franco-Prussian War began in the summer of 1870. German troops laid siege to France, and Napoleon III floundered. A new French government formed but failed to save Paris, which surrendered in January 1871. The war ended on May 10, 1871.

Bloody conflicts escalated when Parisians withdrew from the new French government to form the Paris Commune. From March 18 to May 28, 1871, terrifying battles took place between the Commune and the government in Versailles. The Commune was suppressed, and almost 60,000 of its members were arrested or killed.

When Cassatt and her friend and fellow artist Emily Sartain traveled to France after the war, destruction was still visible. They heard stories, such as the one recorded by Sartain in a letter to her father, of the violence and bloodshed:

Helmick gave terrible accounts of the revolting cruelties of the Versailles troops on entering Paris (they were shooting women and children in crowds right by his house),—and Czapek, a Swiss watchmaker on the Castiglione said the same thing of what he saw in front of his house—He says they dragged women with their heads in the dirt, their legs over their shoulder,—and killed innocent people without any provocation.[1]

1. "Emily Sartain to John Sartain, Borgo Riolo No. 21, January 1, 1872," in *Cassatt and Her Circle, Selected Letters*. Ed. Nancy Mowll Mathews. New York, NY: Abbeville Press, 1984, p. 90.

Dangerous Times

Cassatt and her mother stayed briefly in Paris before striking out for Rome, Italy. Mary rented a studio there and spent six months learning from a French artist. Studying in Rome meant studying the works of antiquity, or ancient times. After the freeing influence of the French artists' colonies, Cassatt's work took a more academic turn. Studying art in Rome was another piece in the standard education of an artist, and Cassatt thoroughly immersed herself in the ancient city.

While the Cassatts were in Rome, political troubles were reaching a boiling point in France. The Franco-Prussian War prompted Americans to return home and avoid the worst effects of the conflict. Many of the American artists in Mary's circle, including Eakins, had already set sail. Mary and her mother returned briefly to Paris in July 1870, and then embarked for America together.

Though Mary was undoubtedly happy to see her family again, she longed for a return to the artistic life she had built for herself in Europe. However, she gladly reconnected

Like Cassatt, Emily Sartain attended the Pennsylvania Academy of the Fine Arts. The two women became close friends and traveling companions.

with students from the Pennsylvania Academy. A friendship with the art student Emily Sartain provided Cassatt with an outlet for sharing and expressing her passion. Emily was the daughter of famous engraver John Sartain and matched Cassatt in her serious commitment to art.

Before long, Cassatt and Sartain were scheming to return to Europe. The Philadelphia art world felt too small for Cassatt, and she was ready to break free as soon as peace in Europe was reestablished. She wrote to Sartain,

> I long to see you [and] have a talk about art. I cannot tell you what I suffer for the want of seeing a good picture, no amount of bodily suffering occasioned by the want of comforts would seem to be too great a price for the pleasure of living in a country where one could have some art advantages.[12]

In the meantime, Cassatt made do with short trips in the United States. She joined her mother for a visit to Pittsburgh and met with the archbishop there. This meeting provided an ideal solution to Cassatt's hunger for Europe. Cassatt would travel to Parma, Italy, and complete two copies of paintings by the Renaissance artist Correggio. The archbishop planned to purchase her finished work for the Catholic Cathedral of Pittsburgh. The commission was a sign of Cassatt's budding professionalism. It was also her ticket back to Europe.

After receiving this exciting news in Pittsburgh, Cassatt visited Chicago, Illinois, with her cousins. She brought two paintings with her, hoping to sell them or at least draw attention to her work. They were hung at a jewelry store in the city, but Cassatt's visit to Chicago was disastrously timed. While she was there, the Great Chicago Fire of 1871 broke out. Cassatt and her cousins escaped unhurt, but her paintings were casualties of the disaster.

The exciting prospect of her Italian commissions no doubt raised her spirits, and Cassatt and Sartain began earnestly planning their travels together. As Cassatt wrote to her friend, "Oh how wild I am to get to work my fingers farely itch [and] my eyes water to see a fine picture again."[13]

A Special Commission

Cassatt was optimistic about the artistic possibilities that would develop once she was back in Europe. She had a great interest in Italian and Spanish art, and the contacts provided by the archbishop could grant her special access to galleries and social circles. He had written her a letter of introduction to use in Italy. Cassatt boasted to Sartain: "when I said I was to have a letter to the archbishop, I believe I was mistaken, I should have said

Cassatt's style in Parma imitated the solid figures and dramatic gestures of the Italian masters, especially Correggio. Cassatt captured the local flavor for this submission to the 1872 Salon.

a letter to *all* the bishops, stamped with the episcopal seal [and] enjoining them *all* to give me aid [and] comfort in every possible way. I think it may prove very useful."[14]

Cassatt and Sartain began the familiar journey to Europe in December 1871. They landed in England, traveled to Paris, and continued on to Parma. A warm reception in Italy allowed both artists to get quickly to work with satisfying results. Cassatt became quite a celebrity, and Sartain wrote to her father about the positive attention:

All Parma is talking of Miss Cassatt and her picture, and everyone is anxious to know her—The compliments she receives are overwhelming—At Prof. Caggiati's reception men of talent and distinction to say nothing of titled people, are brought up to be presented, having requested the honor of an introduction … I shine a little, by her reflection.[15]

Cassatt and Sartain enjoyed each other's company as traveling companions. Sartain, although an accomplished engraver, was a new student of painting. She and Cassatt provided helpful critiques for each other, appreciating and learning from the great Italian artworks in Parma. They remained together in Italy until April 1872, when Sartain traveled to Paris to begin more formal studies under a French painter. Cassatt completed her copy in Parma, packaged it, and sent it to the archbishop. She then continued on to Madrid, Spain, and Seville, Spain, for a close view of the Spanish masters.

In her typically enthusiastic style, Cassatt wrote gushing letters to Sartain about the wonders of Spanish art. She repeatedly urged her friend to join her in Spain, writing, "oh Emily *do do* come, you will never regret it."[16] The Spanish school presented a bold and intense style of art that deeply resonated with Cassatt.

Inspired, Cassatt spent six months in a rented studio in Seville. She set about the usual work of hiring models and obtaining supplies. A difficult painting for the next year's Salon absorbed her time and involved some unexpected challenges. In a letter to Sartain, she jokingly complained, "My present work is … three figures life size half way to the knee. All the three heads are foreshortened and difficult to pose so much so that my model asked me if the people who pose for me live long."[17]

After Spain, Cassatt continued her tour of European art. She briefly returned to Paris for the yearly Salon where one of her Spanish-themed paintings was on display. Following her triumph at the Salon, she made stops in Holland, Belgium, and Rome, devoting time to studying the particular artistic styles of each location. The spring of 1874 found her back in France, visiting Paris and Villiers-le-Bel. Cassatt had spent so much time praising Spain and Italy and criticizing the French school of art that many of her friends were

Single Ladies

Lydia Cassatt's arrival in Paris, although undoubtedly comforting to her sister, had social motivations. It would have been improper for Mary to live entirely independently. Having her single, older sister as a companion at home and on outings protected Mary's reputation as a lady.

The city of Paris was an unfriendly place for an unaccompanied woman. Her mere presence in certain areas could dangerously damage her reputation. The rules may have relaxed by 1874, but this comment from Jules Michelet in 1860 gives an idea of the challenges faced by women in Paris:

How many irritations for the single woman! She can hardly ever go out in the evening; she would be taken for a [sex worker]. There are a thousand places where only men are to be seen, and if she needs to go there on business, the men are amazed, and laugh like fools. For example, should she find herself delayed at the other end of Paris and hungry, she will not dare to enter into a restaurant. She would constitute an event; she would be a spectacle: All eyes would be constantly fixed on her, and she would overhear uncomplimentary and bold conjectures.[1]

1. Quoted in Norma Broude and Mary D. Garrard, eds., *The Expanding Discourse: Feminism and Art History.* New York, NY: IconEditions, 1992, PDF e-book.

surprised to see her settle there. Having completed her tour, Cassatt felt it was necessary to be back in Paris, the powerful center of Modern art.

Return to Paris

While she was in Holland and Belgium, Cassatt had been joined by her mother. Then, her sister, Lydia, arrived to keep her company and help her settle into a new studio and apartment in Paris. Lydia filled the role that her mother, Haldeman, Sartain, and other friends had played in earlier days: They made Cassatt's travels through Europe safe and respectable. The two sisters took great care in decorating their apartment and entertaining visitors. After so many years of travel, Cassatt established her own home.

Cassatt was 30 years old and had been roaming from city to city for the past 8 years. As a more mature artist, it was time for her to settle down and secure financial success for her work. Her artistic reputation had been strengthened by time in Italy and Spain, and since her disappointment in 1869, all the works she submitted to the Paris Salon had been accepted. Despite her evident talent, Cassatt had alienated herself from the academic art world in

Paris with her openly critical views. This set her at a disadvantage in achieving financial success in Paris.

Nevertheless, Cassatt's friends were excited to see her return. Her passion for art made her a stimulating member of any circle, even when that passion was expressed in strong and often negative opinions. Sartain celebrated Cassatt's return to Paris when she wrote to her father:

Oh how good it is to be with someone who talks understandingly and enthusiastically about Art … I by no means agree with all of Miss C's judgments, — she is entirely too slashing, — snubs all modern Art … but her intolerance comes from earnestness with which she loves nature and her profession.[18]

Cassatt began to adjust her style to fit in with the fashionable art of Paris. She focused on more conventional techniques, trying to attract the commissions of traveling Americans who wanted portraits as souvenirs. She also completed two portraits of her sister and another of a little girl for the Salon of 1875. To Cassatt's horror, the portrait of Lydia was refused.

Breaking Point

The refusal of Lydia's portrait seemed to confirm Cassatt's worst suspicions about French academic art and the Salon. Many of the jury's judgments were subjectively based on connections with the artist. In addition, the jury had a strongly conservative bias and set formulas for artistic success. Cassatt tested these formulas by darkening the background of Lydia's portrait to conform with conventions. When the altered painting was resubmitted to the Salon of 1876, its acceptance provided sufficient proof for Cassatt of the jury's narrow and rigid vision. Always skeptical, Cassatt now became completely disillusioned with the Salon.

Refusal by the Salon damaged Cassatt's friendships as much as her pride. Her embarrassing failure in 1875 made her touchy and defensive. A major argument erupted with Sartain as a result. Sartain's conservative tastes had annoyed Cassatt ever since her return to Paris. This rupture proved fatal to their friendship.

Fortunately for Cassatt, she had Lydia's company and supportive new friends. In 1873, Cassatt had been introduced to Louisine Elder (later Havemeyer) from New York. Eleven years younger, Havemeyer respected Cassatt's artistic philosophy and was eager to learn her opinions. In Havemeyer's memoir, she recalled,

I felt then that Miss Cassatt was the most intelligent woman I had ever met, and I cherished every word she uttered and remembered almost every remark she made. It seemed to me no one could see art more understandingly, feel it more deeply or express themselves more clearly

than she did.[19]

Despite Cassatt's resistance to the Salon, she had depended on and benefited from its support. When both of her submissions for the 1877 Salon were refused, Cassatt found herself at odds with the most powerful artistic force in France. If she was to be a successful professional artist, she would either have to give in to the Académie's smothering demands or find another, more radical approach.

Cassatt was not the only artist refused by the Salon. Other artists who felt similarly stifled were gradually breaking away from academic art and defining a new approach. Cassatt had missed a significant moment in French art while she was working abroad. In 1874, a group of artists bypassed the Académie. Instead of submitting to the Salon, they organized and publicized an independent exhibition that was arranged without bureaucratic juries. This group of independent artists — the Anonymous Society of Painters, Sculptors, Printmakers, etc. — became known as the Impressionists. They provided the alternative artistic route that would allow Cassatt to prosper as an artist in her own right.

CHAPTER THREE

Joining the Impressionists

The first exhibition of the Anonymous Society of Painters, Sculptors, Printmakers, etc. opened on April 15, 1874. These artists revolted against the Académie's juries and awards. The photographer Nadar loaned the Society his recently emptied studio as an exhibition space. For a month, visitors could view more than 200 works by 30 different artists. Exhibitors included Pierre-Auguste Renoir, Claude Monet, Edgar Degas, Alfred Sisley, Paul Cézanne, Camille Pissarro, and Berthe Morisot.

As a revolutionary challenge to the Salon system, the first exhibition attracted excited attention. Members of the public came in droves. Some art critics exercised their most disagreeable remarks, ridiculing and attacking the art and artists. The critic Louis Leroy jeeringly called the artists "Impressionists" because their work seemed like unfinished sketches or impressions, especially compared to the highly polished art of the Salon. His name for the movement stuck, though some of the artists preferred to be known as the Independents.

Although the Impressionists exhibited together, their unity as a group initially had more to do with their opposition to the Académie than it did with a particular artistic style. Their work represented a variety of aims and means. As Impressionism developed, it became identified with distinctive techniques and subjects. A sketchy approach resulted in visible brushstrokes and dabs of color that

Claude Monet's painting Impression, Sunrise *provided the inspiration for the movement's popular name. His style gives the sense of a fleeting moment in time, quickly captured on canvas.*

Modern Life

For the Impressionists, depicting modern life meant focusing on the world as it was seen by the artist. For so long, academic art's fascination with the classical world had resulted in historical, symbolic, or timeless scenes and figures. In contrast, Impressionist works could be easily recognized as belonging to the current day. The men and women in Impressionist paintings wore the latest fashions. They walked down the wide boulevards of Paris that viewers of the paintings would easily recognize. They participated in new leisure activities. Impressionist landscapes featured evidence of new industry and technology: Trains wound through the backgrounds, and factory smoke rose in the distance.

In addition to modern subjects, the Impressionists used modern materials. The introduction of paint tubes granted greater mobility to artists. Traditionally, paints were carefully mixed using powders and oils in the studio. The invention of tin tubes that could hold bright new shades of oil paints made it easier for artists to work *en plain aire*, or outside. Most Impressionists also used smaller, more transportable canvases. They followed leisure-seeking Parisians as they took the train to popular bathing and boating spots or enjoyed sunshine in the garden. The Impressionists immersed their art in modern life.

resolved into an image. A focus on the effects of light was characteristic of the Impressionists. Their bright colors created a strong contrast to the dark and subdued works of the Salon. A range of subject matters, including landscapes, garden parties, theater scenes, and café society, signaled a dedication to depicting modern life in both the city and the country.

When the second Impressionist exhibition was organized in 1876, Cassatt was back in Paris. Many members of the original group—including Monet, Renoir, Degas, Sisley, Pissarro, and Morisot—exhibited, with the addition of a few newcomers, such as Gustave Caillebotte. The works were hung at the gallery of art dealer Paul Durand-Ruel. Again, some critics' judgments were harsh. The public showed less interest than they had in the first exhibition. The fate of the Impressionists was still deeply uncertain, but at least one art critic was optimistic. Edmond Duranty published an essay called "The New Painting" that thoughtfully considered the fresh appeal of the Impressionists:

It is really because it is a great surprise in a period like this one, when it seemed that there was no longer anything left to discover, when preceding periods had been analyzed so much, when we seem stifled beneath the mass and weight of the creations of past centuries, to see new ideas suddenly spring up, a special creation. A young branch has developed on the old tree trunk of art. Will it cover itself with leaves, flowers, and fruits? Will it extend its shade over future generations? I hope so.[20]

The Turning Point

Degas and Cassatt had been touched by each other's work before they ever met. When Degas saw Cassatt's paintings at the Salon of 1874, he exclaimed to his friend, "Here is someone who feels as I do."[21] For Cassatt's part, she remembered passionately admiring Degas's works exhibited in a Paris gallery window: "I used to go and flatten my nose against that window and absorb all I could of his art. It changed my life. I saw art then as I wanted to see it."[22]

Cassatt convinced Havemeyer to purchase one of Degas's pastels in 1875. Havemeyer had to borrow from her sisters in order to come up with the necessary 500 francs. The occasion was deeply significant for all three individuals. For Degas, this was the first time his work had been bought by an American. For Havemeyer, it was the primary installment in what would become a large and significant art collection. For Cassatt, it initiated her important role as advisor to American collectors.

The two artists finally met at Cassatt's studio in 1877. They were introduced by a mutual friend whom Cassatt had met in Belgium. Cassatt later recalled Degas's invitation to join the Impressionists after she faced more rejection from the Salon:

That was when Degas made me promise never to submit anything to the Salon again, and to exhibit with his friends in the group of the Impressionists. I agreed gladly. At last I could work absolutely independently, without worrying about the possible opinion of a jury! I hated conventional art. I was beginning to live.[23]

Cassatt recognized a new and powerful artistic direction in the work of the Impressionists. However, spurning the Académie was an incredible gamble. After several years of uncertainty and compromises, Cassatt chose an artistic direction that would give her the freedom she longed for.

In Cassatt's new pursuits as an Impressionist, Degas provided a generous source of guidance and support. The two artists shared a defining artistic drive that ruled and directed their lives. As peers, they pushed and encouraged each other to experiment with new techniques and effects. They maintained their friendship for the rest of their lives despite frequent disagreements. Cassatt and Degas were both hot tempered and critical—an explosive combination sometimes. Still, throughout their personal arguments, they always held each other's art and skill in high regard.

Absolute Independence

After receiving Degas's invitation to join the Impressionists, Cassatt visited the third Impressionist exhibition. The artists had transformed an apartment into an exhibit hall for one month. Cassatt regarded the walls filled with brightly painted studies of the modern world. The next time the Impressionists exhibited, her work would hang alongside theirs.

Cassatt began preparing. She adopted a lighter color palette, left behind the romantic genre paintings of academic art, and trained her focus on modern figures. She no longer had to cater to the demands of the Salon jury. In fact, in order to exhibit with the Impressionists, artists were not allowed to submit to the Salon. Cassatt had full artistic freedom to explore the themes and styles that interested her.

In Cassatt's Little Girl in a Blue Armchair, *Degas's influence is visible in the spacious background and unusual vantage point that takes the child's view into perspective. According to Cassatt, Degas even touched up the canvas.*

Edgar Degas

Edgar Degas and Mary Cassatt had a great deal in common. They were both born into wealthy, socially respected families. They both committed themselves to studying the Old Masters and incorporated traditional values of line, composition, and draftsmanship in their work. They experimented with various art types, including oil painting, printmaking, and pastels. Unlike the majority of the Impressionists, Cassatt and Degas focused their art on figures rather than landscapes. An interest in the human form and its range of expressive gestures dominated in their art.

Many of Degas's works can be grouped together by their modern subjects. Degas painted scenes from cafés, theatres, horse races, and backstage activities at the ballet. Women bathing or working provided other important motifs, or themes, in his work. Degas explored his themes thoroughly, believing, as he put it, "It is essential to do the same subject over again, ten times a hundred times. Nothing in art must seem to be chance, not even movement."[1]

Degas's focus on ballet dancers resulted in more than 1,500 works. This pastel demonstrates Degas's signature use of a cropped scene, asymmetrical composition, and focus on the movements and gestures of the female body.

1. Quoted in Eric Protter, ed., *Painters on Painting*. Mineola, NY: Dover Publications, 1997, p. 127.

Katherine was very happy with her Impressionistic likeness in Reading "Le Figaro". It was one of the first paintings displaying Cassatt's new style with a lighter color palette.

One of the first works Cassatt completed in her new style was *Reading "Le Figaro"*, which was a portrait of her mother, Katherine. Cassatt's parents and her sister, Lydia, moved permanently to France in 1877. Lydia had gone back and forth between Paris and Pennsylvania several times, but poor health prevented her from joining Mary in 1876. The Cassatts were most likely eager to keep as much of the family united as possible, provide proper companionship for Mary, and stretch their financial resources. Lydia's health provided another reason for the family to be close to fine European doctors.

The Cassatts rented an apartment together in Paris, and Mary rented a separate studio where she worked during the day. She was under pressure from her parents to cover the expenses of her studio, models, and supplies using her income as an artist. A great deal was riding on her Impressionistic debut. Still, Robert wrote in a letter to his son that "Mame [the family's nickname for Mary] is again at work as earnestly as ever [and] is in very good spirits."[24]

Fortunately for Cassatt, *Reading "Le Figaro"* was a success. Her mother was an especially modern figure, not just in her clothing and attitude, but in her reading material. *Le Figaro* was a Parisian newspaper that explored current political themes. Her mother's intense focus on the paper portrays her as an intelligent and serious subject, interacting with the modern world she is a part of. An American art critic praised *Reading "Le Figaro"* in glowing terms, writing, "It is pleasant to see how well an ordinary person dressed in an ordinary way can be made to look, and we think nobody … could have failed to like this well-drawn, well-lighted, well-anatomized, and well-composed painting."[25]

At the fourth Impressionist show, Cassatt submitted 11 works that were similar to *Reading "Le Figaro"* in their lighter color palettes, strong compositions, and focus on figures. The exhibition opened on April 10, 1879. All 11 of Cassatt's paintings and pastels were shown at the exhibit and seen by nearly 16,000 people. In addition, Cassatt and all the artists involved were able to turn a profit. The exhibit included works by Degas, Monet, Pissarro, Caillebotte, and Paul Gauguin. Cassatt was 34 years old, and she had found her niche in the Parisian art world.

A Woman's View

The 11 works Cassatt exhibited in 1879 took female figures as their main subject. Her women were shown either out at the theater or pursuing a quiet occupation, such as reading, at home. These subject choices reflect several important factors in Cassatt's work as a female artist.

The Impressionist artists used their canvases as a window into the modern world. However, many aspects of that world were closed to women. The cafés, brothels, and dance halls that featured so prominently in Degas's work would have been taboo themes for a respectable woman. A double standard was at play: It was perfectly acceptable for male artists to turn their attention, often unwaveringly, to nude women subjects; it was socially unacceptable for women to depict a nude man. Even nude female subjects were controversial for a female artist.

Cassatt had joined a revolutionary camp of artists while living an alternative lifestyle as a mature single woman, but her subjects appear surprisingly tame to today's viewers. As museum curator Laurence Madeline said, "Mary Cassatt, whose independence and feminism were beyond dispute, built her entire oeuvre [collection of work] around the feminine and intimate subjects expected from a woman painter."[26] While male artists concerned themselves with the excitement of modern, urban life, the women were largely limited to traditionally feminine spaces.

Domestic spaces suitable for women to represent included parlors, gardens, and balconies. Proper public spaces were mainly limited to parks and theater boxes. Art historian Griselda Pollock calls these areas the "spaces of femininity."[27]

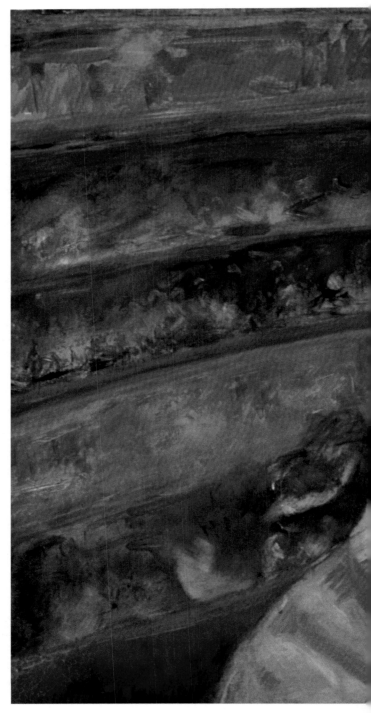

A Corner of the Loge *(also known as* In the Box*) features fashionable women in a theater box. This was an acceptable setting for a painting by a woman such as Cassatt.*

Several of Cassatt's theater scenes highlight the ways women see and are seen in public. Some of her theater figures appear awkward and uncomfortable under the watchful eye of the audience, and by extension, the painting's viewers. The young girls in *The Loge* sit in shy silence, aware of the gazes directed their way. They appear more concerned with their performance as ladylike young women than they are with the evening's entertainment.

On the other hand, *In the Loge* shows an assured,

Cassatt's Impressionistic dashes and dabs of paint in The Loge *convey the varied materials and textures of the scene while also exploring the figures' thoughts and reactions to their environment.*

mature woman. She is actively looking out from the loge, or theater box, where she sits. Her intent attitude is unconcerned with a man in the background who has pointed his opera glasses in her direction. The fan, instead of shielding the woman's face as it does in *The Loge*, is poised unused in her hand. She leans forward and focuses all her energy on looking ahead, careless of the attention she might attract. Her figure may be a stand-in for Cassatt herself, who made her way as an artist by intentionally and actively looking at the world around her.

The woman's modest dress in In the Loge *indicates that she is at a daytime performance. These performances often featured a lecture and were especially appealing to educated women.*

Male artists also had free access to these subjects, which were particularly attractive to Impressionists as scenes of modern life. As a woman, Cassatt turned a sympathetic gaze on the feminine arenas and the women who inhabited them. Although Cassatt painted spaces familiar to her as a woman, the late art historian Charles Harrison offered an important reminder that her paintings are more than a simple recording of her life:

> We should not assume, however, that Cassatt simply painted what she saw around her. Rather her work may be understood as a deliberate and crafted representation of the lives of middle-class women at the turn of the nineteenth and twentieth centuries, as those lives might be realistically imagined—which is to say as they might be imagined by a woman rather than a man.[28]

In her early years as an Impressionist, Cassatt repeatedly used the theater as a setting for female figures. The theater was a popular Parisian attraction. In the 1880s, about 500,000 people attended the theater in Paris at least once a week. The women pictured by Cassatt are finely dressed for an encounter with high society. At the theater, the audience was as much on display as the production was. Gaslights illuminated the elegant space and were kept lit during the show, allowing the audience to see each other. Cassatt used this environment to explore the roles women played in society.

Impressionist Influences

Many male Impressionists also turned their artistic gaze on the feminine spaces Cassatt was interpreting. Renoir focused several canvases on women at the theater. Monet painted gardens and verandas peppered with female figures in frothy modern dresses. As Cassatt exhibited her work alongside the Impressionists, she was able to share ideas, techniques, and friendships with her male counterparts.

Opportunities for stimulating and even heated conversations about art had always attracted Cassatt. She now found herself in a circle of artists marked by similar passion and ambition. Mathews is confident that Cassatt could have held her own when, "for the first time [she] found people whose own biting, critical, opinionated attitudes matched her own."[29]

Cassatt had long admired the work of Manet. Although Manet continued to submit to the Salon instead of the Impressionist exhibitions, Cassatt's engagement with the group would have brought her in closer contact with him. These newfound connections were affirming and inspiring. Robert Cassatt wrote to

Female Impressionists

Although Cassatt was the only American in the Impressionist group, she was not the only woman. Like Cassatt, the artist Berthe Morisot came from a privileged background. She was born into a well-to-do family that encouraged her interest and studies in art alongside her sister, Edma.

Morisot also greatly admired Manet's work. She became a close friend of the artist, posing for him and eventually marrying his brother Eugène. Despite his admiration for her work, Manet gave an idea of the limitations facing female artists when he wrote to a friend: "I am of the same opinion as you, the two Morisot sisters are charming. It's unfortunate that they are not men. As women, however, they could serve the cause of painting, if each were to marry an *académicien*, and sow discord in the camp of these senile old men."[1]

Fortunately for Morisot and Cassatt, the Impressionist artists (especially Degas, who invited both women to join the group) were more open-minded about women's possibilities in the arts. Morisot began collaborating with the Impressionists at their first exhibition. The artist Marie Bracquemond also joined the Impressionists, participating in three of their exhibitions.

1. Quoted in Laurence Madeline, "Into the Light: Women Artists, 1850–1900," in *Women Artists in Paris 1850–1900*. New York, NY: American Federation of Arts, 2017, p. 8.

Alexander about Mary's affiliation with the Impressionists:

The thing that pleases her most in this success is not the newspaper publicity, for that she despises as a rule—but the fact that artists of talent and reputation and other persons prominent in art matters asked to be introduced to her and complimented her on her work.[30]

In addition to her close working and personal relationship with Degas, Cassatt developed a lasting friendship with Pissarro. The two exchanged letters and admired and critiqued each other's work. Another relationship blossomed with her fellow female Impressionist Berthe Morisot. Focusing on similar scenes of feminine life, Morisot participated in all but one of the Impressionist exhibitions.

This new group of peers would likely have overshadowed Cassatt's friends and acquaintances among the American artists. Cassatt was the only American member of the Impressionists. By joining them, she separated herself not only from the rhythms and structures of French academic art, but also from the group of American expatriates. Cassatt was redefining her art and her social circle all at once.

Independent Exhibitions

A fifth Impressionist exhibition was organized and opened in April 1880. Again, Cassatt included portraits and images of women engaging in domestic activities such as reading, working on handcrafts, and entertaining friends. She adopted Degas's use of unusual viewpoints and positioned the viewer of her works close to their subjects. The space of the canvas was divided asymmetrically, and the scene was cropped, giving a feeling of closeness and immediacy. Cassatt's masterful brushwork allowed her to explore the effects of light and texture. In *The Tea*, Cassatt richly depicts a variety of textures: the shiny silver tea set, the patterned sofa, and the delicate fashions, soft hair, and rosy skin of the women.

In addition to paintings, Cassatt also exhibited pastel drawings and several prints in 1880. She had begun printmaking with Degas's encouragement, tools, and printing press. These works were undertaken as a

The Tea *depicts a woman at home with a visitor who is wearing gloves and a bonnet. The nature of the women's conversation is left open to the viewer's imagination.*

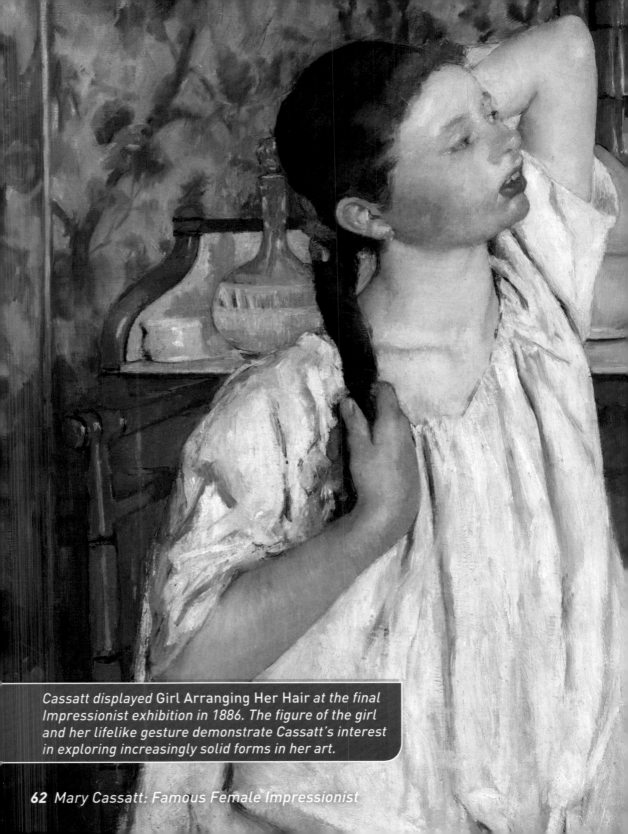

Cassatt displayed Girl Arranging Her Hair at the final Impressionist exhibition in 1886. The figure of the girl and her lifelike gesture demonstrate Cassatt's interest in exploring increasingly solid forms in her art.

collaborative project with Degas and Pissarro. Despite Cassatt's diligent work in learning the new techniques, Degas did not complete his contribution, and their planned journal failed. Instead, eight of the etchings Cassatt had prepared were included in the 1880 exhibition.

The lukewarm reception of Cassatt's work in 1880 was replaced with glowing reviews at the sixth Impressionist exhibition in 1881. Eleven of Cassatt's pastels and paintings were included. These works were strongly influenced by the Cassatt family. Lydia posed for three of the paintings. A summer visit from her brother Alexander and his family in 1880 had provided Cassatt with young models. Her niece Elsie posed for a portrait, and Cassatt captured a sweet image of her mother reading to her grandchildren. When the Cassatts returned to the countryside the next year, Katherine playfully wrote to her grandchildren, "there are so many places to play hide [and] seek in that we shall long to have you all with us [and] your Aunt Mary counts on painting out of doors [and] wishes she had you all there to put in her pictures."[31]

As a group, the Impressionists had been in a state of constant change since their founding.

Rivalries and disagreements sprang up frequently, and artists moved in and out of the group. In the seventh exhibition in 1882, these disagreements affected Cassatt. In protest to changes in the group, Cassatt and Degas withdrew from the exhibition.

The next exhibition did not take place until 1886. This was the eighth exhibition and would prove to be the last. Cassatt played a primary, organizing role. Robert wrote a letter to his son describing all of Mary's practical efforts to make the exhibition possible:

Mame has been working very hard lately preparing for their Exhibition which has been finally arranged [and] fixed for opening 15th May — They have secured a very central position, [and] at a reasonable rent ... Degas and his friend Lenoir Madame Manet (Morisot) [and] Mame — are the parties who put up the money for the rent [and] are responsible for all deficiency's in expenses, [and] are entitled to all profits if there are any (needless to say they do not hope for or expect any).[32]

After all the upheaval among the Impressionists, their exhibition flopped. It seemed that Impressionism was waning. Already, Cassatt's style had begun to drift in new directions. Her figures and their settings were gaining substance, unlike many weightless Impressionist images. Cassatt embraced the independence of the Impressionist exhibitions when she was 34 years old. Now she was 42, and she was ready to take an even larger step in the direction of her unique artistic vision.

Family Life

The developments in Cassatt's professional life were accompanied by significant family changes. Letters from the Cassatts in France to the families of Alexander and Gardner, Mary's brothers in Pennsylvania, chronicle the summer travels, social visits, art news, and regular housing searches that characterized their life. They also provided frequent health updates that prove the assertion Katherine wrote to her son, "so you see we are not a robust family."[33]

Although each member of Mary's family in France suffered periods of ill health, Lydia's case was the most severe. She had been diagnosed with Bright's disease, a fatal kidney disease that plagued her for most of her adult life. Mary nursed her during the worst times of her illness and nurtured their close relationship. To the family's despair, Lydia died in Paris on November 7, 1882, at age 45. The tragic event left Mary depressed, lonely, and unable to return to her art.

It was difficult to recover her passion and drive. When she did resume work, her father wrote, "Mame has got to work again in her studio, but is

Lydia had been Mary's most faithful model, such as in the painting Lydia at a Tapestry Frame. Throughout the changes in Lydia's health, the pair shared quiet companionship as Lydia posed with her work or while reading and Mary painted.

not in good spirits at all. One of her gloomy spells … All artists, I believe, are subject to them."[34]

For the rest of her life, Mary's work was regularly interrupted by poor health within her family. Mary was a dutiful daughter, laying aside her work to nurse her parents and accompany them on trips to warmer locations. These periods of illness and worry were exhausting for Mary. After her mother suffered a serious illness, she wrote to her brother Alexander and closed with, "I am thoroughly worn out and scarcely know what I am saying."[35]

The visits of Mary's brothers and their families provided welcome periods of reunion. Alexander and his wife had four children who visited their grandparents and aunt regularly. Mary became close friends with her brother Gardner's wife, Jennie. Family relationships and close friendships sustained Mary through the difficult period after Lydia's loss and the growing responsibility she held in caring for her aging parents.

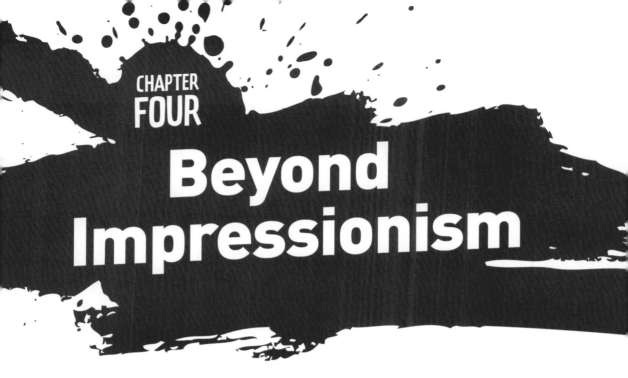

CHAPTER FOUR

Beyond Impressionism

Without regular exhibitions with the Impressionists to look forward to, Cassatt began scouting opportunities to publicize and sell her work. In 1886, her dealer Paul Durand-Ruel organized the first international exhibition of the Impressionist artists in America. Cassatt helpfully provided contacts with the American collectors in her circle, and her brother Alexander loaned key works for the event. The following year, he expanded his operation in New York City by opening a gallery.

Durand-Ruel had been an unshakeable friend to the Impressionists since 1871 when he met Monet and Pissarro in England. In the following years, he had helped the Impressionists

unify as an artistic movement by facilitating their shows, purchasing their works, and promoting their visionary talent in London, Paris, and now in America. He hoped that New York would be key to achieving a vastly wider audience and market for the Impressionists.

The show was composed of 289 works by Cassatt, Degas, Manet, Monet, Pissarro, Morisot, and Renoir. With stunning success, it captured the attention of the New York art world. It also provided much-needed financial stability for Durand-Ruel, who had staked nearly all his resources on the success of the Impressionists. As Cassatt's market expanded to include a larger pool of American collectors, her mother wrote that "Mary is

Children Playing on the Beach, *which was part of the last Impressionist exhibition, is representative of Cassatt's style in depicting children. The closely framed scene emphasizes the children's healthy glow and natural pose.*

at work again, intent on fame [and] money she says, [and] counts on her fellow country men now that she has made a reputation here."[36]

At the time of the American show, Cassatt's art was gradually changing. Leaving behind the Impressionistic subjects of parlor and theater scenes, she began to earnestly study women and children together. In 1888, she made a sketch of her sister-in-law Jennie and her infant son. Children had appeared occasionally in Cassatt's earlier portraits and studies. However, from this point on, the interactions between women and children became a central theme in her work.

Exploring Printmaking

Since her introduction to printmaking by Degas in 1880, Cassatt had diligently worked at the craft. She had always loved a challenge and mastering the multistep process of printmaking became a favorite activity. In 1889, she wrote to Pissarro about their shared interest in printmaking: "Come [and] see me when you are in Paris [and] we will talk over an exhibition, it is time we were doing something again."[37]

The previous winter, Cassatt and Pissarro had joined the Société des Peintres-Graveurs Français. This group exhibited at Durand-Ruel's gallery in Paris in 1889 and 1890. When they planned their 1891 show, they stunned Cassatt and Pissarro by restricting group membership to French artists. This banned Pissarro, who was Danish, and Cassatt from participating.

Cassatt was offended by the exclusion, and she brought her complaints to Durand-Ruel. The dealer proposed a compromise: Cassatt and Pissarro would exhibit simultaneously with the Society, but in a separate gallery. Although her pride remained wounded, this allowed Cassatt to reveal the prints, pastels, and paintings that had absorbed her attention over the past year.

The set of prints featured women in the midst of activities as ordinary as trying on clothing, sealing a letter, and bathing. Richly patterned clothing, wallpaper, and furniture filled the flattened space of the prints. Cassatt's advancing skill as a designer and colorist had a chance to shine. Pissarro wrote a glowing review. "You remember the effects you strove for at Eragny?" he asked his son who was also a printmaker. "Well, Miss Cassatt has realized such effects, and admirably: the tone even, subtle, delicate, without stains on seams: adorable blues, fresh rose, etc."[38]

In order to arrive at this point, Cassatt devoted large quantities of time to experimenting with printmaking. With Degas, she had learned the unconventional practice of merging different printmaking methods and materials. The main techniques she experimentally combined included etching, aquatint, lithography, and monotype.

Printmaking Processes

The various printmaking techniques create lines and transfer ink in different ways. For example, in one method, an etching is drawn onto a coated copper plate. An acid solution is applied to the plate, and the acid bites into the copper where the lines have been drawn. Ink can then be applied. It collects in grooves created by the acid. In a press, the ink is transferred to paper. The number of prints is limited since the grooves in the plate wear down with each printing.

Creating colored prints requires multiple plates. It can be tedious, expensive, and time consuming. In contrast, Pissarro was deeply interested in Cassatt's innovative techniques. He wrote to his son, "I watched her make color prints of her aquatints. Her method is the same as ours except that she does not use pure colors, she mixes her tones and thus is able to get along with only two plates."[1]

Cassatt combined drypoint and aquatint, using multiple plates to produce In the Omnibus. *Aquatints are etchings that create tone with evenly distributed dots of ink. Drypoint is an engraving process in which a sharp needlelike tool is used instead of acid to make grooves in a copper plate.*

1. "Camille Pissarro to Lucien Pissarro, Eragny, April 25, 1891," in *Cassatt and Her Circle: Selected Letters.* Ed. Nancy Mowll Mathews. New York, NY: Abbeville Press, 1984, p. 220.

Woman Bathing represents one of only two images created by Cassatt with partially nude women. The medium of the print resulted in a subdued, and therefore acceptable, depiction of nudity.

Cassatt spent 9 months printing and hand-inking the 10 compositions 25 times each. After so much painstaking work, it is no wonder she was eager to exhibit the results. Cassatt's sophisticated work inspired Childe Hassam, a fellow American artist, to declare that "hers is the most notable name in the history of the graphic arts."[39]

Japonisme

Cassatt drew inspiration for her colored images from a collection of Japanese prints she saw in 1890. Responding to the trending interest in Japanese art and culture called *Japonisme* (love of the Japanese style), the École des Beaux-Arts showcased the work of Japanese printmakers in an extensive exhibit. Cassatt was entranced by the *ukiyo-e* style of artists such as Kitagawa Utamaro, who used wood block prints to decoratively portray Japanese life.

Japanese influences had already defined many features of Impressionism. A focus on modern life strongly echoed the fundamental ideas of Japanese art and *ukiyo-e*. Degas was an early observer and collector of the artistic style. He had been integrating Japanese qualities into his art since the 1860s. His cropped compositions and extreme angles and viewpoints, later adopted by Cassatt, were inspired by Japanese prints. An interest in decorative Japanese objects and materials such as fans, kimonos, and silks was also popular in France and influenced the work of Degas, Monet, Gauguin, and others.

After seeing the Japanese prints, Cassatt wrote to Morisot and urged her to visit the exhibit. She sent a plea similar to the one she addressed to Sartain when she was fascinated by the Spanish artists: "Seriously, you must not miss that … You who want to make color prints, you couldn't dream of anything more beautiful. I dream of it and don't think of anything else but color on copper."[40]

Cassatt's dreams were realized as she committed herself to color printmaking with renewed vigor. Her engagement with the modern world deepened through Japanese-inspired prints. She reduced everyday scenes into the simplified lines of a printmaker. Then, she filled the images with planes of decorative patterns. Cassatt's strong grasp of perspective and composition ensured her success as a printmaker.

Modern Woman

The artistic triumph of her colored prints stoked Cassatt's hunger for art. Unfortunately, her newfound passion for printmaking was soon checked by another deep loss. That year, Mary and her parents observed their usual custom of spending the summer in the countryside. Robert increasingly felt the effects of age and ill health throughout their stay. When the family returned to their Paris apartment, the 85-year-old was desperately weak. He passed away on December 7, 1891.

Mourning the loss of her father, Cassatt needed a distracting new project. She was soon offered an opportunity

Utamaro was part of the ukiyo-e school in Japan that used block prints to represent what they called "images of the floating world." Like Cassatt, Utamaro focused on the everyday activities of women.

三月義佐昔ハ三日之かをらゝせ
上代巳日城男ひ水邑之出て搖
子庵六八周の代小娌リ狨狨に
雄略天皇上巳小水邑之御幸
なりゝるゝあり欲小
ゝ邑をちりけふゝて搖此荒盛リ
上ろこの日ゝなもゝさゝらん

The colorful patterns of Cassatt's print The Letter seem to animate the image. However, they are contained within the flattened surface and simple lines that make up the print.

that would fully absorb her thoughts and attention. Two American women called on Cassatt the following spring. They were organizing the Woman's Building for the World's Columbian Exposition that would be held in Chicago in 1893. They commissioned Cassatt to complete a mural for the building.

Cassatt had never undertaken a mural. She recorded her reaction to the proposal in a letter to Havemeyer:

I am going to do a decoration for the Chicago Exhibition. When the Committee offered it to me to do, at first I was horrified, but gradually I began to think it would be great fun to do something I have never done before and as the bare idea of such a thing put Degas in a rage and he did not spare every criticism he could think of, I got my spirit up and I said I would not give up the idea for anything. Now one only has to mention Chicago to set him off.[41]

Two large murals would face each other. The theme on one end would be *Primitive Woman*, while Cassatt's theme would be *Modern Woman*. She set to work planning and designing her nearly 60-foot (18.3 m) long composition.

Cassatt bestowed the modern women of the mural with modern clothing and modern ideas. Her models wore gowns designed by Charles Frederick Worth, the period's most celebrated women's fashion designer. Cassatt followed her usual tendency of choosing healthy rather than conventionally pretty models. As she said, "Everyone has their criterion of beauty. I confess that I love health and strength."[42] Her scenes depicted healthy women of all ages pursuing truth, education, renown, and the fullness of life. Bright colors and decorative borders enlivened the subject. The tone of the piece was cheerful and foretold a bright future for women. Unfortunately, the *Modern Woman* mural was lost after the Exposition. The mural is linked to Cassatt's other work from that time with similar multigenerational scenes, such as the one depicted in *Child Picking a Fruit*.

Even before Cassatt's mural was mounted, it was criticized. Cassatt enthusiastically defended her project against skeptics. She wrote, "An American friend asked me in rather a huffy tone the other day, 'Then this is woman apart from her relations to man?!' I told him it was. Men I have no doubt are painted in all their vigor on the walls of other buildings."[43]

Cassatt's vision of *Modern Woman* did not resonate with typical Americans. Her work was heavily criticized and misunderstood. In addition, her lack of experience with murals led to misguided choices. At such a great height, the bright colors of the mural appeared garish and inharmonious with the rest of the building.

Completing the mural opened Cassatt's eyes to a surprising streak of conservatism among Americans. Having interacted with the forward-thinking organizers of the Woman's Building, such as Bertha Honoré Palmer and Sara Hallowell, she had not expected to encounter so many unenlightened opinions about women. She wrote to Hallowell, "After all, give me France. Women do not have to fight for recognition here if they do serious work. I suppose it is Mrs. Palmer's French blood which gives her organizing powers and determination that women should be *someone* and not *something*."[44]

Women and Children

For Cassatt, being "someone"—an artist—meant sacrificing other possible identities. She had resolved to remain single in order to pursue her passion and profession. She was proud of this choice, her successes, and her independence. Although Cassatt's family provided a financial security net, her own income had increased steadily through the years. Cassatt had designed and enthusiastically adopted a life for herself, and her primary identity was as an artist.

The companionship of Lydia and her parents had enhanced that path. Since her father's death, Mary and her mother were closer and more dependent on each other. Katherine was frequently ill, causing Mary to worry and postpone work. In the last year of Katherine's life, they split their time between Paris and the country house Mary had purchased the year before. Katherine died in their new home in Beaufresne, France, on October 21, 1895.

The void left by her mother's death may have spurred Mary's renewed focus on women and children—with a sense of longing, perhaps for the experience of motherhood that Cassatt had forfeited, or for the loving, motherly relationship she had recently lost. For the rest of her career, Cassatt's work was almost exclusively concerned with scenes of mothers and caretakers guiding,

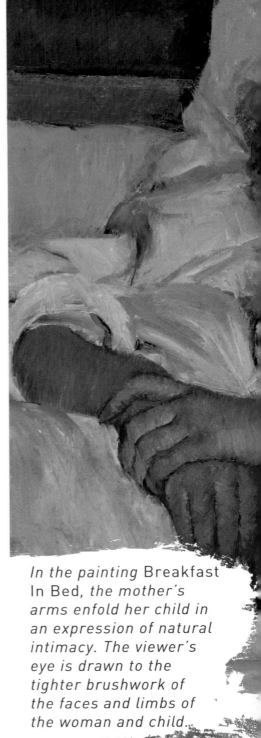

In the painting Breakfast In Bed, *the mother's arms enfold her child in an expression of natural intimacy. The viewer's eye is drawn to the tighter brushwork of the faces and limbs of the woman and child.*

comforting, and tending to children. Although she adopted it late in her career, Cassatt's work is mainly identified with this theme.

Cassatt was following a universal theme, and the further she pursued it, the more traditional and sentimental her representations became. The resulting studies were popular with a wide audience during Cassatt's day, just as they are today. Harrison noted of her changing style, "it appears that the specific types of composition and effect that interested her could only now be captured by recourse to well-rehearsed precedents and techniques."[45] Cassatt's artistic style had followed an arc away from classical traditions. Now, she began to produce images with clear echoes of Renaissance art.

Solo Shows

Without regular Impressionist exhibitions to look forward to, Cassatt sought other venues for her work. In 1893 and 1895, Durand-Ruel organized Cassatt's first solo shows

"Cult of True Womanhood"

The idea that women's primary identity is tied to the home is known as the "cult of true womanhood." It was embraced by many of Cassatt's contemporaries as a way of celebrating the morally pure work of tending to the home and raising children.

Many of Cassatt's earlier works challenge this notion by showing women of all ages engaged in independent and sometimes intellectual activities. However, after 1880, Cassatt repetitively focused on childcare. Still, her interest in women and children does not necessarily support the virtues of homelife. As an artist, Cassatt recognized that scenes of women and children offered a particularly rich realm of human interactions to study. She represented constructed scenes, often of unrelated, hired models.

Cassatt gives a woman the reins in A Woman and a Girl Driving *from 1881. She leads the way forward as her groomsman sits idly behind. The young girl's glance is fixed straight ahead.*

Cassatt (left) is seen here with the daughter-in-law of her friend and promoter, Durand-Ruel. By this time, Cassatt had become an acclaimed artist in both France and America.

in Paris and New York. With his help, Cassatt was steadily shipping works to New York to be quickly sold. To meet the demand, she continued producing images of women and children.

In 1898, Cassatt made a trip to the United States for the first time in more than 20 years. She stayed with her brothers' families and old friends such as Havemeyer. Cassatt was able to see an exhibition of her work in New York. Along the way, she visited Philadelphia and Boston, Massachusetts; earned commissions for 20 portraits; and was introduced to artists and collectors. She also formed new friendships, including with the Pope family and their daughter, Theodate.

New connections must have helped to heal the loss of many of her closest artistic peers in France around that time. Morisot had died in the winter of 1895. In November 1903, Pissarro also died. As Degas suffered from ill health and fading vision, his characteristically testy personality grew more pronounced. He was difficult company even for close friends such as Cassatt.

Despite these losses, Cassatt remained faithful to the principles that had drawn the artists together. She saw her art move from the margins of the art world to the center of attention. In America, Cassatt's art received recognition. Though grateful for the attention, she steadfastly refused to accept rewards beyond the sale of her work.

In one polite but firm letter, Cassatt declined an award and explained, "I, however, who belong to the founders of the Independent Exhibition must stick to my principles, which were no jury, no medals, no awards."[46] When she was awarded cash prizes, Cassatt requested they be transferred to young artists who would benefit most. In declining a spot on a jury panel, Cassatt modestly wrote, "I would never be able to forgive myself if through my means any pictures were refused. I know too well what that means to a young painter and then why should my judgement be taken? Or any one [else's] for that matter in the hasty way in which pictures are judged."[47]

Cassatt's style was changing. She was making a name for herself that was increasingly independent of the Impressionists. However, her artistic philosophy remained firmly rooted in the movement that had seen her potential and inspired her devotion as a young artist.

Dark Days

A new sense of fame and fortune enveloped Cassatt. She continued to travel and work, enjoying the recognition she had longed for. However, when her brother Gardner died in 1911, just five years after Alexander's death, Mary and her work began to falter.

Mary had traveled with Gardner and his family on a trip to

Egypt that resulted in her brother's fatal illness. The travel and resulting tragedy took a physical and emotional toll on Mary, who was already suffering from diabetes. Her health remained fragile for the rest of her life, resulting in long periods when she was unable to work.

Beginning at age 69, Cassatt was also limited by cataracts. She underwent several surgeries but did not have significant improvement in her vision. She was unable to paint from 1904 on. She could read and write only with great difficulty.

Her personal struggles were matched by the global troubles of World War I. Cassatt was deeply affected by the uncertainty and loss that characterized this time. Havemeyer had devoted herself to working for suffrage (women's voting rights), and Cassatt encouraged her and tried to convert others to the cause. In helping Havemeyer organize an exhibition to support suffrage, Cassatt wrote to a potential contributor:

> *Of course, every question is subordinated [something of lesser importance] to the war, but never more than now was suffrage for women the question of the day—the hope of the future. Surely, surely, now women will wake to a sense of their duty and insist upon passing upon such subjects as war, and insist upon a voice in the world's government!*[48]

Cassatt no longer had access to the usual solace of hard work. In one bleak letter, she wrote of the doubts and sorrow that overwhelmed her: "In looking back over my life, how elated I would have been if in my youth I had been told I would have the place in the world of Art I have acquired and now at the end of life how little it seems, what difference does it all make."[49]

Cassatt's place in the world of art was secure,

For the last years of her life, Cassatt enjoyed the pleasures of quiet country life. She is seen here in the gardens at the Church of St. Trophimes in Arles, France, in 1912.

as evidenced by the interest young artists took in her. They traveled to the country to seek Cassatt's advice and hear her stories of taking the art world by storm. She acted generously, despite her intimidating presence, toward the next generation.

On a final visit to Cassatt before her death on June 14, 1926, one of these younger artists noted the undiminished strength of spirit that had carried Cassatt so far in life. George Biddle wrote admiringly, "Miss Cassatt as usual did the talking. Her mind galloped along ...What abysses and reinforcements of courage and life and enthusiasm still lay hidden inside that frail body."[50]

CHAPTER FIVE

An Enduring Legacy

In 1880, Mary wrote to her brother Alexander, "Did you get the photographs I sent you? I only sent them to give you an idea of Degas style, I don't like to buy anything for you, without your having some idea of what it would be like."[51] She was playing a role that came naturally to her—freely offering her opinions on the merits of artwork and encouraging others to see them, too.

Alexander had risen to success with the Pennsylvania Railroad and secured an incredible fortune for himself. With Mary's help, he became an avid collector of Modern art. Mary played the role of scout, seeking out quality works and informing Alexander about them before the costs went up. She had a keen sense for investing and the art market.

Cassatt also perfected this role with Havemeyer and her husband. Cassatt had high hopes for their collection. She praised it in a letter to her friend Theodate Pope, "I consider they are doing a great work for the country in spending so much time [and] money in bringing together such works of art, all the great public collections were formed by private individuals."[52] Cassatt's prediction came true when Havemeyer willed many of her works to the Metropolitan Museum of Art.

By advising collectors and activating an American market, Cassatt provided crucial support to her fellow artists. She not only promoted the work of the Impressionists, she also bought it herself. In this way, she helped provide necessary resources so that the artists could continue working. As a contributor and promoter, Cassatt forged a path for Impressionism in America.

The Advent of Modernism

The Impressionism that Cassatt promoted so passionately ultimately ushered in a new era of Modern art. Impressionism made an important and irreversible break with traditional art, and the next generations of artists took full advantage of the groundwork the Impressionists laid for bold artistic experimentation. Like the Impressionists, they also largely rejected the Salon and jury systems and found innovative ways of displaying and promoting their work.

Although Cassatt was a devoted Impressionist, she was reluctant to accept the new directions chosen by their successors. Cassatt had always been hypercritical of other artists. She had ruined friendships by dismissing her peers as amateurs or imitators. In Cassatt's opinion, the heights reached by Impressionism would be difficult to match. When Degas died in 1917, she mourned the loss both personally and professionally. She wrote in a letter, "he was my oldest friend here, and the last great artist of the 19th Century — I see no one to replace him."[53]

The artistic movements that immediately followed Impressionism included Symbolism, Fauvism, and Cubism. Cassatt seemed unimpressed by the avant-garde art evolving around her in France. She communicated a characteristically cutting judgment of the new art in a letter to her niece: "No sound artist ever looked except with scorn at these cubists and Matisse."[54] She may have been more sympathetic to the American Impressionism movement that sprang up in response to their French counterparts. Despite her complaints, it was Cassatt's work as an Impressionist that eased the transition from traditional to Modern art.

Femininity or Feminism?

As a female artist, Cassatt's works have been subjected to close analysis. She took women and children as her subject matter at a time when few other options were open to female artists. Instead of being limited, Cassatt used the tools available to her to explore and push her art. Her subjects should not overshadow the revolutionary techniques and philosophies she employed in depicting them. The late feminist art historian Linda Nochlin warned against this tendency: "In any case, the mere choice of a certain realm of subject matter, or the restriction to certain subjects, is not to be equated with a style, much less with some sort of quintessentially feminine style."[55]

It is apparent from Cassatt's life that she deeply valued her own independence. She defied expectations for women and joined a growing number of her peers who wanted to live as professional artists. Cassatt was clear that

Degas's portrait of Cassatt, although she disliked it, captures her intelligence and personal force. These qualities enabled Cassatt to become a persuasive advisor and advocate for the Impressionists.

Representation of Women Artists

Even a century after Cassatt's remarkable and groundbreaking career, women artists struggle for representation and appreciation. Roughly half of the artists today are women. Unfortunately, female artists statistically earn lower wages than males. Women in the United States generally make $20,000 less than men in the arts.

The work of women artists is also less visible. At major museums and galleries, an overwhelming number of exhibits feature male artists. The permanent collections of these museums in America and Europe are also dominated by men's work. Only 3 to 5 percent of that work has been produced by women. In 2012, only 2.7 percent of art books were devoted to female artists. Fortunately, women are steadily gaining ground in leadership roles at museums. Despite the advances made since Cassatt's lifetime, female artists are a long way from gaining equal footing with men.

As one of the best-known female artists, Cassatt's work and connections with the Impressionist movement have inspired museum exhibits around the world. Two of her paintings are seen here (far left and far right) as part of the "Impressionism, Fashion, and Modernity" exhibit at the Metropolitan Museum of Art in 2013.

she did not want her work judged by the typically lower standards for weighing women's work. She did not wish to be thought of as a woman painter, but merely as an artist.

As a devoted suffragist, Cassatt used her artistic influence to support the cause. In 1915, she helped Havemeyer organize a special exhibition in New York to benefit women's suffrage. The exhibit placed the works of Cassatt and Degas side by side with the Old Masters from Havemeyer's collection. During Cassatt's lifetime, women in the United States—but not in France—would achieve the right to vote.

It seems surprising that so many images of women performing traditional roles were presented by an uncommonly independent woman. However, Cassatt was a complex person with a rich background of experiences and opinions. It may be misguided to limit her works to one view or set of motivations. What is evident is that, regardless of the social

expectations and limitations surrounding her, Cassatt lived the life she wanted for herself and created work that she found fulfilling and exciting.

Inspiring Women Artists

Aspiring female artists were undoubtedly influenced by Cassatt's highly visible success as a professional artist of serious subjects. By allying herself with the most revolutionary artistic movement of her time, Cassatt proved that women could also ride on the cusp of artistic change. She was part of a generation of artists who elevated women's work from the hobby painting of portraits and decorative arts to the pursuit of more expansive subjects and styles.

Even after Cassatt's success was evident, opinions about the inferiority of women's art abounded. Women were discouraged from serious artistic pursuits. Their ambitions were dismissed by critics such as Thadée Natanson in 1896 who wrote, "Between sewing a bodice and composing a painting, from *la toilette* and a work of art, there is a distance that the brains of these ladies—an inferiority of essence or lack of education—cannot span."[56]

Cassatt envisioned a future in which artists would be given opportunities for education and judged on their talent rather than their sex. Already, changes were in motion that would allow greater opportunities for female artists. Even the École des Beaux-Arts had opened its doors to women. Cassatt actively advocated for the young female artists who came into her circle. Most importantly, she set an international precedent with her own success.

Permanent Images

At 15 years old, Cassatt had a vision of herself as an artist. Her unshakable faith in her own potential and passion to achieve and advance as a professional directed every major decision she made from that point on. She was driven and uncompromising, and she knew the full cost of each of her accomplishments. Once, when describing her artistic process to Havemeyer, she summed up the trials and triumphs of her work as an artist:

I doubt if you know the effort to paint! The concentrations it requires to compose your picture, the difficulty of posing the models, of choosing the color scheme, of expressing the sentiment and telling your story! The trying and trying again and again, and oh, the failures, when you have to begin all over again! The long months spent in effort upon effort, making sketch after sketch … After a time, you get keyed up and it 'goes,' you paint quickly and do more in a few weeks than in the preceding weary months. When I am en train nothing can stop me and it seems easy to paint, but I know very well it is the result of my previous efforts.[57]

To the outside world, Cassatt's work seemed to be always *en train*, creating its own unstoppable momentum and leading Cassatt on to new heights. She lived to be 82 years old and saw the world around her and the definition of art shift dramatically during her lifetime. Still, it was not until nearly 100 years after her death that a Cassatt retrospective (an exhibition of an artist's past works) was held in a French museum.

In 2018, the Jacquemart-André Museum in Paris held an exhibition called "An American Impressionist in Paris" in which more than 50 of Cassatt's works—including prints, pastels, oils, engravings, and drawings—were displayed. Pieces for the exhibition were loaned from museums across the United States and France, as well as from private collections. This retrospective was the first time Cassatt's works had been brought together in a single exhibition.

Cassatt's works, such as Young Mother Sewing, often depicted thoughtful young girls.

In the spring of 2019, Cassatt's work would once again be displayed alongside that of her French Impressionist counterparts, including Degas and others who were featured in the earliest Impressionist exhibitions. It was announced that this exhibition, titled "Across the Atlantic: American Impressionism through the French Lens," would be on display at the LSU Museum of Art in Baton Rouge, Louisiana, from March 8 through June 9, 2019. It is clear, even today, that the story Cassatt told through her art continues to appeal to audiences around the world.

Notes

Introduction: An Uncommon Artist

1. Quoted in Nancy Mowll Mathews, *Mary Cassatt: A Life*. New York, NY: Villard Books, 1994, p. 200.

Chapter One: Early Life

2. David G. McCullough, *The Greater Journey: Americans in Paris*. New York, NY: Simon & Schuster, 2011, p. 211.
3. Mathews, *Mary Cassatt*, p. 12.
4. Quoted in Mathews, *Mary Cassatt*, p. 24.
5. Mathews, *Mary Cassatt*, p. 20.
6. Quoted in Mathews, *Mary Cassatt*, p. 58.

Chapter Two: Studying the Masters

7. "Eliza Haldeman to Alice Haldeman, Courances, February 1867," in *Cassatt and Her Circle: Selected Letters*. Ed. Nancy Mowll Mathews. New York, NY: Abbeville Press, 1984, p. 40.

8. "Eliza Haldeman to Alice Haldeman, Courances, February 1867," in *Cassatt and Her Circle*, p. 41.
9. "Eliza Haldeman to Samuel Haldeman, Courances, April 24, 1868," in *Cassatt and Her Circle*, p. 51.
10. "Eliza Haldeman to Mrs. Samuel Haldeman, Courances, March 8, 1867," in *Cassatt and Her Circle*, p. 43.
11. "Mary Cassatt to Lois Cassatt, Beaufort sur Doron, Savoie, August 1, 1869," in *Cassatt and Her Circle*, p. 61.
12. "Mary Cassatt to Emily Sartain, Hollidaysburg, June 7, 1871," in *Cassatt and Her Circle*, p. 74.
13. "Mary Cassatt to Emily Sartain, Hollidaysburg, October 27, 1871," in *Cassatt and Her Circle*, p. 77.
14. Quoted in Mary Elizabeth Boone, *Vistas de España*. New Haven, CT: Yale University Press, 2007, p. 76.

15. Quoted in Mathews, *Mary Cassatt*, p. 79.
16. Quoted in Mathews, *Mary Cassatt*, p. 82.
17. Quoted in Boone, *Vistas de España*, p. 96.
18. Quotes in Kirsten Swinth, *Painting Professionals: Women Artists & the Development of Modern American Art, 1870–1930.* Chapel Hill, NC: University of North Carolina Press, 2001, p. 55.
19. Louisine W. Havemeyer, *Sixteen to Sixty: Memoirs of a Collector.* Ed. Susan A. Stein. New York, NY: Ursus Press, 1993, pp. 269–270.

Chapter Three: Joining the Impressionists

20. Edmond Duranty, "The New Painting: Concerning the Group of Artists Exhibiting at the Durand-Ruel Galleries (1876)," in *Impressionism and Post-Impressionism, 1874–1904: Sources and Documents.* Ed. Linda Nochlin. Englewood Cliffs, NJ: Prentice-Hall, 1966, p. 4.
21. Quoted in "Mary Cassatt and Edgar Degas," Philadelphia Museum of Art, accessed on June 29, 2018. www.philamuseum.org/exhibitions/2003/200.html.
22. Quoted in Barry Schwabsky, "Transient States: On Mary Cassatt," *Nation*, June 5, 2013. www.thenation.com/article/transient-states-mary-cassatt/.
23. Quoted in Lauren Thompson, "Mary Cassatt & Edgar Degas: Learn About the Two Artists in *Her Paris & Degas*," Denver Art Museum, January 5, 2018. denverartmuseum.org/article/mary-cassatt-and-edgar-degas.
24. "Robert Cassatt to Alexander Cassatt, Paris, October 4, 1878," in *Cassatt and Her Circle*, p. 138.
25. Quoted in McCullough, *Greater Journey*, p. 354.
26. Laurence Madeline, "Into the Light: Women Artists, 1850–1900," in *Women Artists in Paris 1850–1900.* New York, NY: American Federation of Arts, 2017, p. 13.
27. Griselda Pollock, "Modernity and the Spaces of Femininity," in *Vision and Difference: Feminism, Femininity, and Histories of Art.* London, UK: Routledge, 1988, p. 259.
28. Charles Harrison, "Morisot and Cassatt: 'A Woman's Painting,'" in *Painting the Difference: Sex and Spectator in Modern Art.* Chicago, IL: University of Chicago Press, 2005, p. 131.
29. Mathews, *Mary Cassatt*, p. 117.
30. Quoted in McCullough, *Greater Journey*, p. 394.
31. "Katherine Cassatt to Katharine Cassatt, 13, Avenue Trudaine,

April 15, 1881," in *Cassatt and Her Circle*, p. 159.

32. "Robert Cassatt to Alexander Cassatt, 14, Rue Pierre Charron, May 5, 1886," in *Cassatt and Her Circle*, p. 198.

33. "Katherine Cassatt to Alexander Cassatt, 13, Avenue Trudaine, December 10, 1880," in *Cassatt and Her Circle*, p. 156.

34. Quoted in McCullough, *Greater Journey*, p. 418.

35. "Mary Cassatt to Alexander Cassatt, 14, Rue Pierre Charron, May 12, 1884," in *Cassatt and Her Circle*, p. 185.

Chapter Four: Beyond Impressionism

36. Quoted in Mathews, *Mary Cassatt*, p. 200.

37. "Mary Cassatt to Camille Pissarro, 10, Rue de Marignan, November 27, 1889," in *Cassatt and Her Circle*, p. 213.

38. Quoted in Michele Slung, "Mary Cassatt Goes to Paris," *Washington Post*, July 29, 1984. www.washingtonpost.com/archive/entertainment/books/1984/07/29/mary-cassatt-goes-to-paris/8e687c7b-da11-4680-b50c-a70d9146c0e7/?noredirect=on&utm_term=.e0a481e93010.

39. Quoted in Griselda Pollock, *Mary Cassatt: Painter of Modern Women*. London, UK: Thames & Hudson, 1998, p. 24.

40. Quoted in Michael Kimmelman, "Review/Art: In Washington, Cassatt's Japanese-Inspired Prints," *New York Times*, June 27, 1989. www.nytimes.com/1989/06/27/arts/review-art-in-washington-cassatt-s-japanese-inspired-prints.html.

41. Quoted in Sally Webster, *Eve's Daughter/Modern Woman*. Urbana, IL: University of Illinois Press, 2004, p. 64.

42. Quoted in "Minds Wide Open: 400 Years of Women Artists," Virginia Museum of Fine Arts, accessed on June 29, 2018. www.vmfa.museum/tours/audio-tours/minds-wide-open-400-years-women-artists/#lKupB4vcdia0ievu.99.

43. Quoted in Julia Pierpont, *The Little Book of Feminist Saints*. New York, NY: Random House, 2018, p. 61.

44. Quoted in "Sara Hallowell to Bertha Palmer, 118 South 20th Street, Philadelphia, February 6, 1894," in *Cassatt and Her Circle*, p. 254.

45. Harrison, "Morisot and Cassatt," p. 144.

46. Quoted in Thomas Streissguth, *Mary Cassatt: Portrait of an American Impressionist*. Minneapolis, MN: Carolrhoda Books, 1999, p. 95.

47. "Mary Cassatt to Harrison Morris, Mesnil-Beaufresne,

August 29, 1904," in *Cassatt and Her Circle*, p. 294.

48. Quoted in Linda Nochlin, "Mary Cassatt's Modernity," in *Women Artists: The Linda Nochlin Reader*. Ed. Maura Reilly. New York, NY: Thames & Hudson, 2015, p. 218.

49. Quoted in Ann Dumas et. al, eds., *The Private Collection of Edgar Degas*. New York, NY: Metropolitan Museum of Art, 1997, p. 100.

50. Quoted in McCullough, *Greater Journey*, p. 456.

Chapter Five:
An Enduring Legacy

51. "Mary Cassatt to Alexander Cassatt, 13, Avenue Trudaine, November 18, 1880," in *Cassatt and Her Circle*, p. 152.

52. Cynthia Saltzman, *Old Masters, New World: America's Raid on Europe's Great Pictures, 1880– World War I*. New York, NY: Viking, 2008, p. 112.

53. "Mary Cassatt to George Biddle, 10, Rue de Marignan, September 29, 1917," in *Cassatt and Her Circle*, p. 328.

54. Quoted in Mathews, *Mary Cassatt*, p. 283.

55. Linda Nochlin, "Why Have There Been No Great Women Artists?," in *Women, Art, and Power, and Other Essays*. New York, NY: Harper & Row, 1988, p. 149.

56. Quoted in Madeline, "Into the Light," p. 6.

57. Quoted in Pollock, *Mary Cassatt*, p. 188.

For More Information

Books

Groom, Gloria, ed. *Impressionism, Fashion, and Modernity*. Chicago, IL: Art Institute of Chicago, 2012.

> In this book, readers learn about the meaningful connections between fashion and modernity and the ways they were represented by the Impressionists.

Madeline, Laurence, ed. *Women Artists in Paris 1850–1900*. New York, NY: American Federation of Arts, 2017.

> This book investigates the artistic achievements of 36 women artists who lived and worked in Paris.

McCullough, David G. *The Greater Journey: Americans in Paris*. New York, NY: Simon & Schuster, 2011.

> For 19th-century American artists, scientists, writers, and politicians, Paris offered an ever-expanding world of culture, thought, and change. This book traces the fascinating journeys of Americans in Paris from 1830 to 1900.

Rubin, James Henry. *How to Read an Impressionist Painting*. New York, NY: Thames & Hudson, 2013.

> Taking a creative approach to understanding Impressionism, this book categorizes and explores Impressionist art by subject matter.

Weidemann, Christiane. *50 Women Artists You Should Know*. Munich, Germany: Prestel, 2017.

> This book chronologically examines the lives and work of 50 women artists who have shaped major artistic movements from the Renaissance to postmodernism.

Websites

Cambridge Contemporary Art: Printmaking Techniques
www.cambridgegallery.co.uk/printmaking-techniques/
> This website from an art gallery in Cambridge, England, teaches a variety of printmaking techniques through clear explanations and illustrative videos.

Heilbrunn Timeline of Art History
www.metmuseum.org/toah/essays
> This website from the Metropolitan Museum of Art features essays about artists and movements throughout art history.

Hill-Stead Museum
www.hillstead.org/
> The family home of Cassatt's friend Theodate Pope has become Hill-Stead Museum. This website allows visitors to view the museum's collection online to see Impressionist works and photographs of Cassatt taken by Pope.

Louvre Museum
www.louvre.fr/en
> The official website of the Louvre museum allows visitors to take a virtual tour of the Louvre and see the spaces and artwork Cassatt studied as she copied the great works of the past.

Mary Cassatt
www.nga.gov/collection/artist-info.1107.html#biography
> The National Gallery of Art's website features a brief biography about Cassatt as well as more than 100 of her paintings, drawings, and prints.

Index

Picture Credits

Cover (screen image) Rawpixel.com/Shutterstock.com; cover (painting) Universal History Archive/UIG via Getty Images; pp. 1, 3, 4, 6, 12, 26, 44, 67, 85, 93, 97, 99, 103, 104 (big paint swatch) Lunarus/Shutterstock.com; pp. 7, 64–65 Fine Art Images/Heritage Images/Getty Images; pp. 9, 52 Private Collection/ Photo © Christie's Images/Bridgeman Images; p. 10 Bequest of Edith H. Proskauer, 1975/Metropolitan Museum of Art; pp. 14–15 Leemage/Corbis via Getty Images; pp. 16–17 Christophel Fine Art/UIG via Getty Images; pp. 18–19, 73 Courtesy of the Library of Congress; pp. 22–23 Hulton Archive/Getty Images; pp. 22, 27, 30, 39, 50, 56, 57, 70, 76, 79, 83, 88 (paint caption background) Jaroslav Machacek/Shutterstock.com; p. 24 Courtesy of the Library of Congress Prints and Photographs Division; p. 27 Bettmann/Bettmann/Getty Images; pp. 28–29 Kiev.Victor/Shutterstock.com; pp. 32–33 Universal History Archive/ Getty Images; pp. 34–35 PHILIPPE LOPEZ/AFP/Getty Images; p. 37 Historic Images/Alamy Stock Photo; pp. 38–39 Art Collection 2/Alamy Stock Photo; p. 45 DeAgostini/Getty Images; pp. 48–49, 56, 62 Everett - Art/ Shutterstock.com; pp. 50–51, 91 H. O. Havemeyer Collection, Bequest of Mrs. H. O. Havemeyer, 1929/Metropolitan Museum of Art; pp. 54–55 Francis G. Mayer/Corbis/VCG via Getty Images; pp. 57, 87 VCG Wilson/Corbis via Getty Images; pp. 60–61 Barney Burstein/Corbis/VCG via Getty Images; p. 68 Ailsa Mellon Bruce Collection/National Gallery of Art; pp. 70, 71, 74 Gift of Paul J. Sachs, 1916/Metropolitan Museum of Art; pp. 76–77 Huntington Library and Art Gallery, San Marino, CA, USA/© The Huntington Library, Art Collections & Botanical Gardens/Bridgeman Images; pp. 78–79 Philadelphia Museum of Art, Pennsylvania, PA, USA/Purchased with the W. P. Wilstach Fund, 1921/Bridgeman Images; p. 80 Siren-Com/Wikimedia Commons; pp. 82–83 Fotosearch/Getty Images; p. 89 STAN HONDA/AFP/Getty Images; back cover vector illustration/Shutterstock.com.

About the Author

Rachael Morlock lives and writes in Western New York. She holds a degree in Art History from Canisius College in Buffalo, New York. Her strong love of art has often prompted exasperated friends and family members to leave her behind in museums. Rachael is a firm believer in reading every museum label.